Kinky Tales

Real stories of my journey

Master Taíno

Kinky Tales

Real stories of my journey

by Master Taíno

Fair Page Media LLC
Springfield, PA

ISBN: 978-0-9989098-8-2

Copy Editor's Note

In a little restaurant, over two decades ago, I fell in love with the boys of Master Taíno's Leather Family. Through them I came to know Master Taíno as my *Nuttah Noshi (Heart Father)*, when I was inducted into the Family several years later. It has been my honor to edit this book of life stories for my *Noshi*.

Gypsie-Ami Offenbacher-Ferris

To all the individuals who have impacted my life and my journey as a Leatherman, a BDSM practitioner, and a Master.

To all those whom I have been able to touch during their respective journeys and allowed me to make a difference in their lives.

To all the slaves who have trusted me and committed to serve this Master for a short or long term.

To my Leather Family.

LEATHER FAMILY

A Leather Family is the
family of our choice, not
an imposed one, but the
one we choose and
embrace.

Master Taíno

Table of Contents

Foreword

You hold in your hands a deceptively slim volume.

This collection of short, personal, stories from Master Taíno can easily be read in an hour or so. Only a few of them are longer than a couple of pages, and some are not even that. But I suggest that you take your time and read each story mindfully—there's more here than you might realize if you just breeze through, something profoundly affirming and, dare I say, potentially transformative.

Some of the stories, like "The Sanctuary," "Straight Firefighter," and "The Boy at the Hoist" are erotic; others, like "The Kilt," are humorous. Some are inspirational, such as "A Master Is Born," "A Three-Decade Secret," and the combination of "Costa Rica" and "Leather Grandpa." And some, including "Men Don't Cry," "Slave Paul," "My Boots," and, especially, "Slave Tommy" are quite moving. All of them are interesting.

While reading interesting stories can be pleasure enough in and of itself, discovering how each of the events and relationships that they chronicle served to develop the author into the man, Master, and kink community leader he is today not only deepens that pleasure, it encourages the reader to appreciate how the stories of their own life have molded and shaped them as well. On the other hand, some readers may be left feeling painfully aware of how much room for personal growth they have. Fortunately, the greatest, if perhaps unintentional, gift of this book is this: What led Master Taíno to reaching his full potential was embracing the truth of who and what he is. That being the case, then the same can be true for anyone, and so to those readers I say, you'll find much reason for hope in these stories. Allow them to be a catalyst for your own self-actualization.

Candor compels me to acknowledge that I've known Master Taíno for 25 years, and we are good friends. I've been personally present for some of the events about which he's written. I'm mentioned in a few of the stories, and I'm indirectly referred to in one or two more. My memory of some of the facts may vary from his, but, as the character Tommy DeVito says in *Jersey Boys*, "Everybody remembers it the way they need to." (That's a musical theatre reference — it's a gay thing.) You'll find that these stories are written in a simple style, as might be expected from someone for whom English is a second language. Many of them contain the occasional mangling of good grammar that is an endearing quality of Master Taino's verbal communication, and if you know him, then you, like me, will no doubt hear his voice in your head as you read each one.

One more thing: It's Master Ty-EE-no, not Master Tee-AH-no. Get it right — as this book amply proves, he deserves that respect.

Master Skip Chasey
Los Angeles, California
June, 2024

Introduction

Leather and kinky friends have previously asked if I had any plans to write a book. I never thought that I would have much to contribute that had not already been written. After I had established my second home in Costa Rica, I thought about the suggestion. I realized that as a retired journalist and kink educator, I have developed the reputation of being a storyteller. When people ask me questions regarding Master/slave relationships or BDSM, I usually respond with a story. Stories . . . *those* I can write. That is normal for me.

So, I started writing stories and that's how *Kinky Tales* emerged. Old age is not good for keeping a good memory and my memory is awful. I kind of forget everything. But the interesting thing is that there are some stories and experiences I have had during my Leather journey that I can remember in vivid detail. These stories, the unforgettable ones, are the ones that I was able to write and collect into this book. Some experiences are funny, unusual and interesting, and some are very powerful. Most of the stories I relate here have an underlying message that I hope will touch my readers as they have touched my life.

Some stories are about people I have lost contact with, so I do not reveal their names. Others have given me permission to include only their first names. But some have allowed me to add their part in the stories. These are very powerful, as well as beautifully complementing my own renditions and the message each one holds.

This book reflects who I am as a person, as a Leatherman, as a BDSM practitioner, and as a Master. Many of the stories relate to my passion and belief in cathartic flogging and the impact it has had on the people who have experienced it firsthand, beneath my flogger.

The Universe guided me to positions of leadership within our Leather, Kink, BDSM, and Master/slave communities, with a mission to promote education as a tool in creating the best community. After decades doing just that I feel compelled to share my stories again with the purpose of leading by example. Mama Vi Johnson, cofounder of the Carter Johnson Leather Library, has said many times that everyone in our community has a story, and those stories are worthy to be shared. Here is mine.

The sad part will be that after the book is published, I will keep remembering other stories that I wish I could have included.

The best part is that many of these tales show something and someone I care about. There is nothing more rewarding for a human being than being able to make a difference, small or big, in another human being's life. That's what life is all about for me.

I hope you, the reader, will enjoy my stories as much as I have enjoyed writing them.

Master Taíno

Photo courtesy of JP Monge

Kinky Childhood

I do have a great many memories of my childhood that I can now associate with my kinky personality. I am convinced that those experiences during childhood have a lot to do with who we are today due to our inherent DNA. For most of us we were born this way, and I have been teaching this ever since.

Movies played a part in my kinky awakening as a child. While growing up in the 60s and 70s, Western movies were very common. I could watch Sunday matinees, two westerns, for only ten cents.

That was the first time I saw men being tied up, over and over, movie after movie. I didn't know why it was exciting in some strange way. That lead to childhood cowboy and Indian games with my friends and trying to tie someone up.

Then there were plenty of Medieval-themed movies with lots and lots of torture scenes. I have never forgotten watching a guy being stretched on the rack. I was jumping on my chair but did not know why. I was reacting to the scene very differently than anyone else was.

In both the Western and Medieval movies, the costumes the men wore were interesting and sexy. At such a young age I knew nothing about sex or kink, yet those characters definitely did catch my attention.

There were other characters that also spoke to my kinky gay side, although again, I did not realize what it was at the time. More than for kink, but for the gay inside me that I still did not know. Like who? The Lone Ranger and Tonto, Cisco Kid and his sidekick, Pancho, and of course, Batman and Robin.

It is amazing the number of Catholic folks, including priests, that I have met in my lifetime who are kinky. Going back to my childhood, I believe that many of the Catholic practices reveal the essence of kink. I see it in other religions as well, Christian or otherwise.

Here are some examples from my own personal memories that I can recall. During my elementary grades in a Catholic School, the nun who was the principal had a thick paddle called "ABC" in her office. She used the paddle on the kids who were sent to her office for misconduct. Each time a classmate was sent to the office I tried to imagine how he was being spanked.

One of my favorite stories the nuns told us was about the saints that used to auto-flagellate themselves. I was nearly jumping out of my chair.

Growing up Catholic, we watched many movies about the passion of Christ every Holy Week. There was kinky stuff in those movies, from the flagellation of Jesus, the crown of spines, and the crucifixion itself. And I must repeat once again the story of my reaction as an altar boy to getting hot wax on my hands while holding a candle during a Good Friday procession. It was such a great feeling that I went home and began to play with candles. I was maybe around twelve years old.

Then came what I consider my first BDSM experience with another boy. When I was around thirteen years old I used to invite another altar boy to enact the Mass. Once, I told him I was tired with Mass, and that we should reenact the Way of the Cross. That became kinkier. Yes, this altar boy had a dirty mind at a very young age, even though I had no idea why.

Then there were the stories of the martyrs. St. Sebastian, almost naked, getting wounded with arrows. St. Stephen getting stoned. St. Peter's crucifixion, head down.

This is what I have learned from these childhood stories. Our kinky hearts begin to wake up when we are exposed to these stimuli. As an adult, I then read a book by a psychologist about how childhood memories reveal things about ourselves. His book validated my theory.

I am free because I am
out. I am free because I
relate to all people.
I am who I am.
If anyone doesn't like it,
deal with it because I am
not going back.

Master Taino

Batman and Robin

Many kinksters appear to be drawn to superheroes during their childhood, and I was no exception. I have had a fascination with *Batman and Robin* since I was a small child, and it was not only because they occasionally got tied up in their hot outfits.

It was mainly due to their unique relationship. I was intrigued with the idea of an older man (Batman) and his young protégé (Robin), living and being together. The same when they were home as Bruce Wayne and Dick Grayson.

I wondered what that relationship was all about. Why did it call to me so very strongly? An older man and a younger one, together. Intriguing, captivating, and stirring.

As with many of my childhood stories, this one was a precursor of who and what I was going to be as a grown man. I have always been attracted to younger men. Within our Leather community we call younger men "boys," although, of course, they are of legal and consenting age.

I have continually identified as the Batman, a dominant and protector of someone younger. Even as a young man still living in Puerto Rico, long before I discovered the Leather community and BDSM, I was drawn to this dynamic. When I was twenty-four, my boyfriend was eighteen. When I was twenty-eight, my second boyfriend was twenty-one and just out of college. This Batman has continued to grow older, and still I am attracted to boys in their twenties and thirties.

I am a fan of recognizing and celebrating milestones. I remain awed, amazed, and very thankful to have had the opportunities to be able to be with younger men, even those decades my junior. Now in my seventies, some of these young men are half a century my junior!

Society at large and even many kinky folks do not always understand my chosen way of life; however, for me there is a very special connection when people with a huge age gap get together. As much as I enjoy their company, as well as teaching and mentoring young men, I find and enjoy their fascination with older men. A mature Dominant brings much to their relationship, from the gray hair and beard to the wisdom, experience, and life knowledge that fosters trust.

Forever *Batman*!

Learning from the Bottom

I joined the Leather Community in 1992 after I ran into an Episcopalian priest friend from the Gay Fathers group. We met up at the DC Eagle, where he told me about his Leather Club.

At the time, like many others, I found the whole Leather scene to be intimidating, even though I was a regular patron at the Eagle. My friend mentioned that his club, the Defenders Leather Levi Club, was a Catholic gay club. That certainly piqued my interest, as I was still struggling with reconciling my sexuality, my sexual orientation, and kinks with my Catholic faith.

Months later I became a pledge to the Defenders Leather Levi Club and eventually a full-fledged member.

I always knew that I enjoyed BDSM, and was very happy to have found that there was another club called SigMa, where I could learn more and practice my kinky techniques. I went to classes and play parties, and found out quickly that I had a lot to learn. I began to study the other dominant guys in the club, and finally asked the president to teach me.

He accepted, and for several months I went to his house to learn from him, or "from the bottom to the top." He did let me know how the flogger felt. However, he never subjected me to a real flogging experience; at least not until the very end of his lessons.

To this day, I am not sure what his intent was, but I knew I wanted to be able to take whatever he dished out on me. It was extremely intense. In my mind I thought I was winning the battle, and I thought I was taking his flogging well. Then, all of a sudden, an internal explosion of emotions occurred, and I ended up sobbing profusely.

My friend held me until I found myself to be in a state of calmness, peace, and pure relaxation. I was in heaven!

That moment changed my life. In that moment I made myself a commitment. If I was going to proceed with my passion for flogging, I wanted those whom I flog to experience what I had just experienced.

Years later, I learned from a fellow master that what I had experienced is called cathartic flogging. The rest is, as they say, history.

Learning Flogging

Early in my journey, after I had relocated from my native Puerto Rico to the Washington D.C. area, I became a regular patron of the DC Eagle Leather bar. This is where I began to take the baby steps leading me into my Leather/BDSM and M/s journey.

The Eagle had a "Dungeon Master." The DM, or Dungeon Master, had a reserved stool at the corner of the bar. He was known as Daddy Jim, a member of the Centaurs MC. I noticed that he always carried a flogger and a set of heavy German handcuffs on his person. Little did I know at the time that years later I would be the Master who entered the Eagle carrying one or two floggers and a set of heavy German handcuffs.

At the Eagle, it was quite common to hear the noise of someone being flogged by Daddy Jim. Many patrons gathered to watch the Master at work. I always got close, not for the show, but to observe what he was doing and how he did it. Those ended up being my first flogging classes.

Something very interesting happened years later. By then, in San Francisco during the pre-Folsom Leather Week, I spent the nights flogging boys until sunrise at a private club. Once, a guy who witnessed me flogging his friend, told me that my style resembled one from a guy he saw in DC some time ago. I realized he was talking about Daddy Jim and told him that I was from DC and that I knew him.

I realized that I had unintentionally learned Daddy Jim's assertive way of flogging and had adopted it as my own. Once, during the Centaurs' Olympia camp event, he did teach me a new flogging stroke. It was a way to flog both the butt and back at the same time through a 180-degree arc.

Throughout the years, I have developed my own style of flogging. I consider watching Daddy Jim at the DC Eagle in my early years my first flogging lessons.

The Sanctuary of the Dark Angel

In 1996 I attended the first Southeast LeatherFest (SELF) held in Atlanta, GA. While at the event, I got to go to an iconic play space, The Sanctuary of the Dark Angel. This venue was owned and operated by the equally iconic Master Doug Harris.

At the Sanctuary I discovered a rack for the first time. This was a piece of torture equipment I had often seen and been intrigued by as a youth, watching my favorite Medieval movies.

During the event I met a boy pup who was tasked to serve me all weekend. After the event was over I decided to visit to the Atlanta Eagle with the pup and a friend from New Orleans, whom I had met up with at SELF. We were chatting at the bar, while the boy was wearing his pup mask and was happily and consensually leashed on the floor next to me.

As I was chatting with my friend I noticed a young man looking at the pup with intensity and awe. This went on for quite a while. I decided to ask the young man why he was so fascinated with my pup. After a brief chat I invited the new young man to join us at the Sanctuary. He told me that he had to check with his boyfriend, and I assumed at that point that it was not going to happen. A few minutes later I heard the young man arguing with his boyfriend; but he returned and headed to the Sanctuary with us.

I had befriended Master Doug at the Sanctuary — a very easy thing to do. The young man, whom I will now refer to as "the boy," got scared when he saw the heavy scenes going on. I told him not to worry, as he would not be doing any of those . . . today. I did not know of course, as I never set predetermined expectations. I just knew the boy was intrigued by what we do.

I tied him to a pole nearby where he could watch how I played with my pup on the rack. My pup was stretched and secured, and I started a hot wax scene with him.

When that scene was completed, my friend and I turned our attention to the new boy. I pulled his pants down and his huge dick popped out. That boy was extremely well endowed for a bottom. Both my buddy and I dropped down and began to enjoy that boy's cock.

I grew fascinated with the new boy and did some bondage, wax, and spanking with him. Eventually, I left my pup with my friend so they could play together. I took the boy to another room where Master Doug had a huge sling. I put the boy on the sling and told him I was going to "rape" him. That's not my usual take as I don't like to have sex in public, but this was not an ordinary day.

I started penetrating the boy hard while he started screaming, "Rape me, Sir!" very loudly and repeatedly, which made the scene hotter than hell. I was so focused on the boy that I did not realize until the end that a whole crowd had gathered around the sling watching us.

After that awesome scene, I sat on a bootblack chair that Master Doug had in the same room. The boy stayed on his knees before me. I decided he had been doing so well all night that he needed a reward. I asked him if he wanted to cum and he answered in the affirmative. I ordered him to jerk off and shoot all his cum on my boots. He obeyed and not a drop fell outside my boots. When he was finished I commanded him to clean his cum off my boots with his tongue. He followed the order beautifully. What a night! What a boy!

This happened in 1996 and I still remember details of this encounter. I often wonder if the boy, now a man in his fifties, also remembers the experience so vividly. My wish is that he not only remembers but cherishes that day, when he was taken to the Sanctuary of the Dark Angel by Master Taíno.

We are called to educate and help those we find in our path. We have to lead by example by living our lives and our relationships with honesty, integrity, and transparency.

Master Taíno

A Shackled Cop

I have so many good Folsom Street Fair stories: interesting and funny experiences while on this journey. Well, except for the individual involved in this story.

Back in the late nineties, while in San Francisco for the Folsom Street Fair, I met a Latino officer from the California Highway Patrol. I did not meet him on the highway. It was in a BDSM play space the night before the Fair.

When we ran into each other, we hit it off right away, only to discover we were both dominants. We spent a lot of time trying to figure out how we could make this work. I won the battle, and he agreed to go as my submissive boy. We played in the dungeon until late and decided to go to the Fair together the next morning. During our time together he did share that he was an officer for CHP.

We met up at 11 a.m. at the Fair as we had previously agreed. I collared and shackled him for the day. During the Fair I ran into another boy who joined us for the rest of the day.

After a very long and fun filled day, we returned to my hotel, followed by dinner. After dinner we prepared to return to Folsom to go to the bars. I was driving my rental car, the other boy was in the passenger seat, and the policeman was in the back, still collared and shackled.

While trying to figure out my directions back to downtown, I made a sharp movement with the steering wheel after realizing that I was not on my exit ramp. A California Highway Patrol cruiser pulled me over immediately. Two officers approached the car. One of them asked me if I had been drinking. I told him I had not had a drink in more than a decade. He then checked my eyes to confirm that I was telling the truth.

Meanwhile, the other officer began to look at the inside of the car with a flashlight. He obviously recognized his colleague in the back seat, all shackled up. The officers did not say anything, as they knew it was Folsom Fair day, but my new friend was pissed because two co-workers found him in that compromising position.

The evening continued with some more fun, but the shackled policeman was not a happy camper. He knew what was going to happen when he reported to work at the station the next morning for work. He related to me later that his co-workers made good fun of him on Monday and for several days later.

Luckily, that did not affect our new friendship. Later he visited me in the DC area. We attended Olympia Leather Camp together, and we saw each other in San Francisco several other times afterward.

Although he has not been the only police officer I have played with, the situation with him made for the best story.

I still have an official CHP handcuff case that he gifted to me.

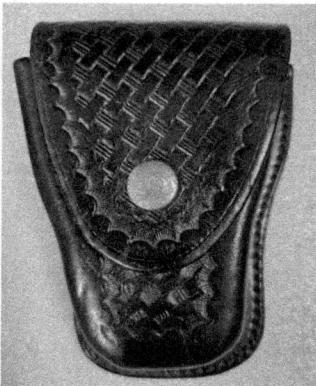

A Master is Born

By 1998 I was immersed in the Leather and BDSM community in Washington, DC, as a member of the Defenders Leather Levi Club and SigMa, as well as around the USA.

Just the year before I had helped our BDSM club, SigMa, procure its first dungeon space. At that time I was still raising my kids, so a dungeon in my house was not an option. I was already active in SigMa, but not in a position of leadership.

In late 1996 SigMa lost the space the club shared with other groups, and a search for a new space began. I joined in the search and found the perfect row house, three blocks from the DC Eagle. I wrote the contract myself, as the club did not have any background experience as a tenant.

To be able to pay for the rent, the group offered special memberships, which provided the member with key access to that little house. We converted it into an awesome two-story dungeon. During that time I immersed myself into a lot of play, day and night, at the new space.

During the summer of 1998 I had one of those *aha* moments after playing with a boy at the SigMa dungeon and waiting for another one to come over. I realized that there was more to this than just BDSM play, or at least I was realizing that I needed more, but was not sure what that "more" was.

A couple of weeks later I went to Lambda Rising, a gay bookstore in the Dupont Circle neighborhood of DC. I always checked the Leather section first, and that evening I ran into a book titled *Ties That Bind* by Guy Baldwin. I didn't have an idea who Baldwin was, but I opened the index, and the first two essays were about Master/slave relationships. I started reading right there, purchased the book, and read it all the way through.

Ties That Bind had the answer to my question. Yes! This is what I had been looking for, and I liked the way Mr. Baldwin, a therapist from Los Angeles, explained the dynamic. I never imagined at that moment how fast the dominoes were going to fall. In better terms, how fast the Universe would push me on this new journey to find my true heart and spirit, my authentic self.

In September of that year I headed to San Francisco to attend my fourth straight Folsom Street Fair, the largest Leather kink event in the world. A Master I had met previously invited me to go to a MAsT San Francisco meeting at the Lone Star Saloon on Harrison Street. There were about twenty-five gay Leathermen discussing M/s relationships, protocols, expectations, and more. As I have done all my life, I jumped right in and asked how to form a group like this. MAsT was founded in San Francisco in 1989, and at the time there were only five chapters in the whole country. I was told the MAsT leaders were in Atlanta.

Being a journalist myself, I started to research and found Master Roger, then the director of MAsT. But while trying to get a chapter for Washington, DC, l learned that Master Roger and others in Atlanta were putting together an event for March, 1999, that was going to be the first educational conference exclusively on Master/slave relationships. More intriguing was that Guy Baldwin, the author of that book I had just read, was the producer of the educational component. Right then I knew I must attend.

On March 17, accompanied by my boy bobby, we drove my new van from Virginia to Atlanta with an overnight stop in Henderson, NC. We arrived at an old Ramada Inn in Midtown Atlanta Thursday afternoon, excited about what would happen that weekend.

For the very first time I received a name badge identifying me as "Master Taíno." About four hundred people attended the event that we called "MAsT 99." There were many classes and panels. Among the people I met that weekend were the two who had inspired my path toward Mastery, Guy Baldwin and Master Steve from Butchmanns. In addition, I met slave david stein, Laura Antoniou, Viola Johnson, Joseph Bean, Master Doug, Ms. Suzan, and many others who became friends right away.

The most memorable "moment" of the weekend was when I attended the reading of the unpublished book *SlaveCraft* by Guy Baldwin. At the end of the reading, along with many others, I approached Guy with my copy of *Ties that Bind* for him to sign. It was the first book ever signed to "Master Taíno." I took the opportunity to engage Guy in a short talk. At the end he pulled a picture of himself from his briefcase, signed it, and gave it to me. I thought he was doing that with everyone, but then he told me that was the only one he brought. Why did he give me his only picture? To this day I don't have an answer, although twenty years later I asked Guy why he did that, and he just replied, "You know."

What I do know is that five years later, because MAsT 99 ended up being a one-time event, I founded the Master/slave Conference (MsC) using the template that Guy Baldwin had created for MAsT 99 — an educational event on Master/slave relationships without BDSM.

Another key moment of that weekend was when Master Steve called me and asked me for my line of questions regarding abuse in many of the panels. I told him that I thought that I had found my calling, but I just needed to be sure that this dynamic was not something to conceal abusive relationships. Master Steve apparently saw something in me and reached out. I realized that he was a wise man, and I began to follow his path and eventually called him my mentor.

MAsT 99 changed my life. That weekend Master Taíno was born.

1999 International Master and slave
Weekend and Contest

997405

Master Taino

Interstate Sodomy

I attended International Mr. Leather (IML) 1999 with two boys: my new slave at the time and a visiting boy/pup from the San Francisco Bay Area. The fun started on our long drive from the DC area to Chicago.

We were driving my conversion van from home to the Windy City. I drove the first four hours until we passed Pittsburgh. Then the boy/pup from the Bay Area took the wheel.

I decided to move to the back seat that converted into a bed with my slave, where we began to have sex. Then we approached the Pennsylvania/Ohio state line and had to stop to pay the tolls. So, I also had to stop the sexual fun in the back of the van until we had left the toll plaza. As soon as we left the toll plaza, the sex continued — but now we were in Ohio.

We started having sex in Pennsylvania and finished in Ohio. At the time sodomy was illegal in both states. What do I call that? I guess it was interstate sodomy!

TOLL ROAD

OHIO

Moravia Rd.

Ohio / Pennsylvania
State Line

PENNSYLVANIA

TOLL ROAD

I learn our history and our traditions, but I am living my leather and my Mastery one way... MY WAY

Master Taíno

A Dream Comes True

I flew to San Francisco to participate in the Folsom Street Fair in September of 1999 for my fifth consecutive year. I returned almost every year during the following two decades. However, Folsom Street Fair of 1999 ended up being the one I will remember forever.

I traveled with my slave at the time, a few days before the Fair. We stayed in the Castro, San Francisco's famous gay neighborhood, hosted by a club brother from the Defenders.

On Thursday we went for lunch at a restaurant right in the heart of the Castro. While we were having lunch, an extremely handsome young man entered the restaurant and sat at a table all by himself. Everyone, including my slave and myself, was mesmerized by the beautiful hunk boy. I believe he was aware of the intense scrutiny, yet he did not even raise his head in acknowledgment. I wondered why such a pretty boy was all by himself.

The next day my slave and I were walking on Castro Street. I saw the same cute boy walking toward us sporting a sharp military hat. Once again he was alone. I nodded to him, and he nodded back. Again, I was surprised that the boy remained alone. I assumed he must be a part of those groups of pretty boys who came to the Fair just to have sex. Still, I found it interesting that he was alone both times we saw him.

Then on Saturday evening, while my slave and I were having dinner at a lovely sidewalk restaurant on Market Street, my slave brought my attention to the same pretty boy as he passed us; again he was alone. Saturday night and still alone? That did not make any sense to me.

Sunday morning I awoke ready for a big day at the Fair. I told my slave that I dreamed that we ran into this boy at Folsom, and I grabbed him.

He answered in good humor: "Yeah right, keep dreaming Sir!"

A pup from San Jose, whom I had met earlier that year during Mid-Atlantic Leather Weekend in D.C., joined us on our way to Folsom Street Fair.

I arrived at the Fair with two boys on leashes. After two or three hours walking around Folsom, we decided it was time for some lunch. While we were walking towards the Food Truck area, guess who was walking towards us? Yes, here he was again, the pretty boy now wearing military pants and a leather harness.

We nodded to each other, but this time I grabbed him, and immediately he got himself in attention position in front of me with his head bowed.

After exchanging some words I pulled another collar and leash from my bag and added him to my other two boys.

We got into the food area, and I sat down to rest my back. The two boys went to get some food, and the new pretty boy kneeled by me. He not only was a gorgeous young man, but had a beautiful smile, tall with a hot body, and somewhat shy. After talking and making out for a while, I pulled his pants down, got him over my knees, and started spanking that awesome round butt, right in the middle of the street. My two boys returned with lunch, and one of them got my camera and took a picture of me spanking the new boy. That picture became iconic and was my profile pic on AOL for a few years.

Obviously, I had to ask him why he was always alone. He told me that he was a Midwest boy but living in Southern

California and staying with an uncle in the Castro while in San Francisco. That's why we were running into him all the time.

He explained that he went to Daddy's bar in the Castro a couple of times, but nobody would talk to him. I knew that many guys are intimidated by a handsome young man. If I had been at Daddy's I would have jumped on him, but we spent our evenings at the Folsom bars and the 15 Association play party.

He stayed with us for the rest of the Fair and for that evening. He agreed to visit us Monday morning, so I left him with a chain collar and told him to wear it locked when he returned to our place the next morning. On Monday his arrival time passed, and I thought he was not going to show up.

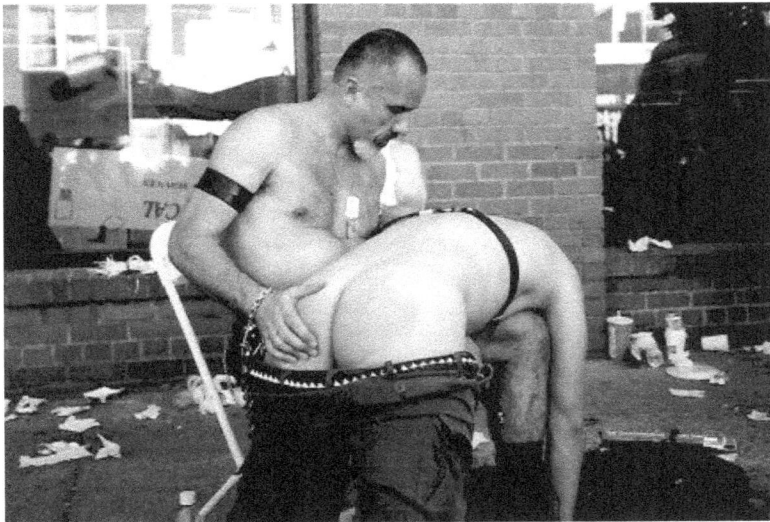

About half an hour later the doorbell rang, and there he was with the collar in his hands, afraid that we might be gone, and he would have been stuck with the locked collar. He apologized for being late and immediately locked the collar, spending the rest of the day with us, including an awesome threesome.

The dream the night before Folsom became a reality beyond my wildest dreams, and the full story is one that I will cherish throughout the ages. I must admit, this story is one of the most memorable highlights of my long Leather journey.

Fisting Tales

Fisting has become a very popular fetish around the world. I've been there and done that as a Dominant/ Top. But I do not like to do this type of play with novices, as I think it is a huge responsibility to fist someone for the first time. However, I do have some entertainingly awesome stories concerning fisting, and here are some of them.

During Mid-Atlantic Leather Weekend back in the nighties, I was staying at the host hotel and ended up fisting two boys at the same time — one with my right hand and the other with my left, as they lay down over the hotel bed, both of their asses up and exposed for me.

On another occasion the Men of Discipline had a party at a house in the Virginia suburbs of Washington, DC, that had been converted into a BDSM dungeon by a professional Dominatrix. The highlight of the night was a fisting demo. The fisted guy was a young man whom I had introduced and trained in consensual BDSM years earlier. After the demo the facilitator told the attendees that the boy was available for more hands. Several attendees fisted him while I waited patiently. When I was ready I knew what I wanted to do. First, I fisted him pushing both of my hands, alternating them in and out. Then I tried to get both hands in together. I got close but never could go all the way. I learned it takes a lot of strength to get both hands inside, and although I was very close, I could not finish the job.

Another experience was with a local DC boy that I knew. On a Saturday evening at the DC Eagle closing time, the boy asked me if we could play. I knew he was heavy into fisting, so I told him it was too late for fisting. He replied that just sex would be enough. So I took him to the nearby SigMa dungeon, put him on the sling, and fucked him good. When done I asked him if he wanted to cum, and he said "yes." I started fingering him while he jerked off. Because his hole was so open, I kept adding fingers to stimulate him.

Suddenly, he grabbed my arm and pushed my hand all the way inside his boy pussy. I was not expecting that, but it was a good feeling that I had never experienced before.

Then there was a Spaniard boy that I met at the Argos Bar in Amsterdam in 1998. He asked me if I was into fisting. I told him I was, but always as part of a BDSM scene. So we agreed to meet at his place the next day. We put together a nice scene, and at the end it was time for fisting. While I was doing the fisting slowly, he suddenly sucked my hand inside his ass. That had never happened before, but the feeling was awesome and very pleasurable.

The last story happened in Berlin in 2005 during their Leather Week, which happens to also coincide with Holy Week. I was with a German slave I had met ten years earlier in San Francisco. We went to Mutschmanns Leather Bar in the heart of the Leather neighborhood in the German historic capital. Unlike in the United States, the European bars have a play area. This one had a full basement for play. I was resting on a sofa with the slave kneeling next to me.

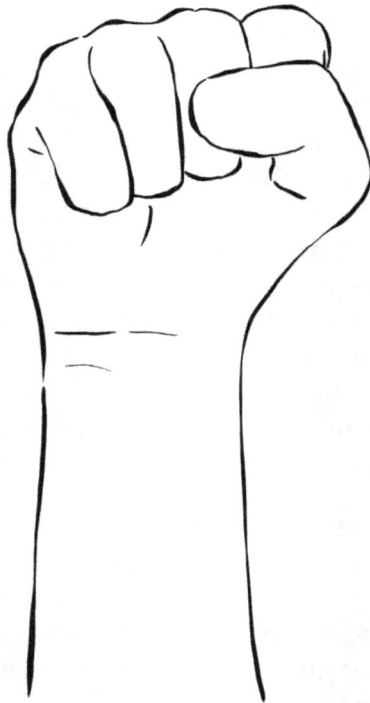

Then a cute boy showed up wearing leather chaps without any jock strap and no shirt. We started making out, and when I touched his cheeks, I noticed he was already lubed up. I asked him if he was into fisting. He replied in the affirmative and laid down on the sofa, spreading his legs. I decided to tease him and put my hand in his ass, which happened to be a big open hole, and in a few seconds my full arm was inside his ass up to my elbow. That was quite an unexpected experience. After I pulled my arm out I had to go to the rest room to wash my entire arm.

Fisting memories that are unforgettable!

I have been blessed with this amazing Leather journey that has allowed me the opportunity to make a difference in so many people's lives.

Master Taíno

The Boy at the Hoist

Right after my fiftieth birthday in the fall of 2000, I traveled to Europe. First I stopped in London and then on to Leather Weekend in Amsterdam. That was my first and only time visiting London.

My friends said that if a Leatherman visited London, he must go the iconic Leather bar, The Hoist. I did go on a Saturday evening, never imagining it was going to be such a memorable occasion.

I entered the bar and immediately saw it was an amazing place. The center area, like an interior deck, caught my attention right away.

While I was checking my jacket, I noticed a gorgeous young man of Asian descent walking across that deck. After leaving my jacket I walked toward the deck and leaned on the railings.

The gorgeous young man, dressed in full Leather, showed up again. He was walking straight ahead, and I was on his left. Suddenly, he looked to his left and saw me. He stopped, turned towards me, bowed his face, placed his arms behind his back, and spread his legs. By doing this, he was telling me without saying a word:

"Here I am Sir, just come and take me."

And that's what I did.

I have never had that kind of experience before. Someone suddenly taking a formal submissive position in front of me, offering himself, was positively amazing.

The young man was a Chinese Canadian music student in London. He was very handsome, with an amazingly built body. He was also very sweet and charming, and he knew his protocols.

We had a wonderful evening together at The Hoist. However, I was not expecting what was going to happen following our encounter that evening.

The following weekend we reconnected with each other again in Amsterdam. We kept in contact, and a month later he let me know that through his college he had a commitment to play in New York City right before Christmas. His original plan was to fly to the U.S. a week early so he could tour the Big Apple.

He asked if instead he could visit me in the D.C. area, where I lived. And, of course, I said yes. After landing at JFK airport, he took the train to DC. We had a blast for the full week. He became very fond of my flogging.

Seven years later in 2007, I was at Folsom Street Fair in San Francisco. That year I settled at the Mr. S booth, flogging boys all day alongside the owner of Mr S, the largest Leather store in the country. While taking a break for lunch, I noticed a gorgeous Asian young man walking close by me, and, like seven years earlier, he turned his head, and our eyes connected. I approached, and he greeted me with a hug.

Then he said: "Sir, nobody has touched my back but you."

That was when I realized who he was. I invited him to the booth of Mr. S, where the boy stripped from his leather, leaving only a leather jock strap on. He was as built and gorgeous as ever. We had a great scene slapping his chest. A picture of that scene made the video in the *San Francisco Chronicle* published the next day. Delightedly, I also proceeded to flog his beautiful back.

Unfortunately, The Hoist closed in 2016. But this is a story I will remember all my life. I hope that boy and I will cross paths again someday.

We are better off
when we can evolve
into better human
beings.

Master Taíno

Slave Tommy

My slave Tommy was one of the first slaves in my service, less than a year after I attended MAsT '99 in Atlanta, GA. According to him, he saw me first during International Mr. Leather (IML) in Chicago. He said he saw me in the vending area and was checking me out (or stalking me). However, it took him several months before he contacted me online. The main reason was that he had been diagnosed with AIDS and almost died that year. After he recovered and started taking his meds, he contacted me, and we arranged for him to visit.

At the beginning I was concerned: his numbers were low, and he could easily get sick again. Finally, with the help of the meds, his numbers went up, and I decided to take a chance on him and offered him his first training collar. He had a house outside Atlanta that he had purchased with his late partner, who had passed away from AIDS-related illnesses a few years earlier. When his mother went through a divorce, slave Tommy welcomed her into his home. We arranged for him to spend about half of the time each month in my home in Virginia and the rest in his house in Georgia.

Slave Tommy was a typical Southern boy — good looking and somewhat skinny from his illness. He embraced the chance to serve me as my slave. At the time we met he was an outsider in the community, looking for casual encounters. He was so proud going to the DC Eagle, the Atlanta Eagle, or to Leather events wearing his Master's collar and sometimes leashed. He loved to wear his leather chaps showing off his small butt with the word "slave" written across it with magic marker. Whenever the letters faded, he would ask me to write it again. He got a real sense of belonging in my family and under my domain.

Sadly, Tommy was very insecure. Watching his body deteriorate and his beauty fade, he was always afraid that I would leave him to find a healthier and prettier boy. As I learned with my adoptive children, I had to constantly reassure him that he belonged with me. He tested me though, and sometimes his behavior brought me so close to uncollaring him. But I have also learned with my adopted children not to give up.

I had to change my goals with him. Instead of trying to make him be the best slave he could be and realizing he was fighting for his life, I decided to give him the best time possible before he eventually passed.

During the first year of our relationship, slave Tommy was mostly healthy. One evening he developed a fever while staying at my house. I kept monitoring the fever until it reached an unacceptably high temperature, so I let him know that I was going to take him to the ER. He did not want to go, saying it was going to be a burden on me. He wanted to drive back to Atlanta the next day to see his doctor. I told him that he was wearing my collar, and I had the responsibility to take care of him, and I was going to take him to the ER. That night was the first signal that his health was deteriorating. Tommy was the second slave I had to take to the ER for illness, even though I was still early in my Mastery (and I took many others to ER after him). Consequently, he could not make the long drive between Virginia and Georgia anymore, but he was able to fly thanks to his slave brother Mike, whom he brought into our family. Mike worked for an airline and provided free vouchers for Tommy's travel.

Getting sick only made Tommy more insecure about our future. He was certain that I was going to get tired of him and drop him. In early 2001 while in Atlanta, Tommy ended up being hospitalized. A couple of weeks later he was back in the hospital. I flew to Atlanta to be with him.

My visit to the hospital was all he needed. He told me later that the fact I had flown to Atlanta to see him made him truly believe that I was not going to abandon him. The rest of the year held ups and downs with his health and more visits to the hospital.

That June, I took him and his slave brother to New York for Folsom Fair East. Tommy was so happy, as it was the first time that he had ever crossed the Mason-Dixon Line. He loved New York and the event. At Leather Pride Night we met Sir Brad, who became a good friend and was very fond of Tommy. Then a month later, I took Tommy back to NYC. While I went to some baseball games, Sir Brad took him to tour the city and fulfilled his dream of visiting the Empire State Building. He was so happy that weekend.

After that, he returned to Atlanta and then September 11th happened. We talked that day, and he could not believe that the Twin Towers, that he had just seen a couple of weeks before, were gone. He also realized that after 9/11, there were not going to be any more travel vouchers, and he would not be able to return to my home. Three days later I called him, and his mother answered the phone. He was not doing well, and the doctors had put him on an IV while at home. If he did not improve by Monday, he was going to be admitted. At the time of the call, I was at a restaurant with my other slave, Dave. I told him to be ready, because if Tommy was admitted on Monday, that would be it. He would not leave the hospital alive. I had the feeling that he did not have the strength nor the motivation to keep fighting.

Tommy was admitted on Monday. On Friday, Dave and I drove to Atlanta and went directly to the hospital. He was so happy to see us and got very animated. His legs were full of liquid. I knew the end was near but stayed hopeful. We chatted with him all the way until midnight.

By the time we returned in the morning, Tommy had taken a turn for the worst.

My last words to him were, "Tommy, we love you," and he mumbled back that he loved us too. I was holding his hand while Dave and Mike were holding my shoulders. We four were connected when at 5:25 that Saturday afternoon, September 22, I sensed his pulse was gone. Our boy left our world. That was one of the early moments in my Leather journey that I realized that my dream of having a Leather Family was real and a good thing.

After Tommy's passing, his mother and two siblings came to us to give us thanks for everything we had done for Tommy. He had two great years at the end of his life, cut short two weeks before his thirty-eighth birthday. That validated my decision to focus on giving him happiness over making him the best slave.

We returned to Tommy's house as needed to clear his room of kink paraphernalia, so his mother would not find his leather stuff. I found his collar, the most important thing. I also found a notebook with some writings. His mother eventually found out some of what Tommy was up to, but she told me that although there were things she could not understand, she did understand the people who had cared for and loved her son.

Upon returning to my home, I began to look through the things I had brought from his room. To my surprise, in the notebook, there was a letter he had written to me. After his death, the boy gave me an immense and meaningful gift.

I am sharing here two letters from Tommy. The first was the one he sent me after his first visit. The second one was the one I found after his death. And finally, I am sharing as well my farewell writing a month after his passing.

A long week

Dear Sir,

Like I said in my previous email, I had 10.5 hours of time to think some thoughts that I wanted to share with you so here it goes.

Sir, thank you for allowing me to come and visit/interview for the position of the houseboy for you and your family!!!

I remember that I was fine on my way up there until about ten miles from your house. Then I got nervous, why . . . . I was scared, didn't really know what I was getting myself into, who I was dealing . . . beginning far from home and not knowing anyone in the area . . . what if something went wrong or didn't work out . . . all of these questions/concerns crossed my mind . . . but I kept driving and arrived at your house. I remember thinking in my mind not long

after I arrived, "this is going to be a long week". In that short time span of a week you showed me not only of life with you and your family, but also showed me something of myself, something deep inside of me was exposed.

You showed me your commitment to the leather lifestyle, the Daddy/boy relationship, and the Master/slave relationship. I have never felt that I was slave material . . . but you seemed to think so. I remember kneeling before you and you placing a big and heavy chain around my neck and locking it on there. I secretly thought, "hell no, this is not staying on all week." I've had chain collars locked on before, BUT, they always came off after "play time" was over. This time the chain/lock didn't not come off. With each passing day I grew prouder and prouder of that chain around my neck and knowing that you placed it there. Finally, this morning, you unlocked the lock and removed the chain from my neck. I felt like I was on the verge of crying. Kinda' like I was being punished for something, but I know that isn't the case Sir.

I feel kinda' lost without the chain/lock on me Sir. I don't have that security of touching the chain/lock and knowing that you are caring/loving/teaching/protecting me. I remember looking at my "potential brothers" with their chain/lock thinking how can they wear them all the time? Now I know "how", it's an honor Sir. The very fact that you saw some potential in me, to place that chain/lock on me, it was now, to me Sir, a honor to wear your chain/lock for that "long week." For me to be viewed by others in the leather community as part of your family was a wonderful feeling and something I was proud of!!!

I miss you and the boys . . . . I felt that I was a part of something during that "long week."

Thank you, Sir, for taking the time to talk with me about any concerns and answer any questions that I had about life with you and your family, my duties and responsibilities to you/family, but mostly for letting me know that I would be loved/cared for just as much as your most senior boy/slave.

Sir, I miss you and being with you and "my potential brothers."

I don't know what the future holds for me in being a part of your family, but at the very least Sir, you showed me more in a short week than most boys/slaves get to learn/experience in a lifetime.

Sir, this is just some of the thoughts in my mind on that "long drive home."

All I can say is Thank You Sir!!!

tommy

An Ever Longer Ride

Dear Sir,

It's now been over a year since i had that long drive back to Atlanta. Little did i know it would be a longer way to the point of where i'm at today. I know that it's been a rough road for me and You.

That first trip up took about 10 hours, and the closer i got the more nervous I became, not knowing what to expect. Yesterday, the trip took only 1.5 hours and a feeling of I can't wait to get here was inside of me.

Over the past year, i know it hasn't been real easy in dealing with me. i offer you my sincere "Thank You" for the patience You have shown.

We have traveled the same roads, although at times it appeared that we had taken different routes, and i will admit that most of the time it didn't seem that i knew where i was going or even why i was going.

A lot of realizations have occurred during the course of the year along with a lot of emotions, frustration, drama, laughter, tears, hugs, and smiles, but most of all, love.

Even with a year that's come and gone, i still have a way to go. i still don't know where all of this journey will lead, but at this point, i am not sure if it's that important that i know.

After Mikey passed on, i ventured down another road that i needed to explore and grow. i learned my spirituality during that time. i now view this past year with You as the same thing, a part of me i needed to explore. Through exploration, one learns about oneself and his surroundings.

You know what January 2001 was like for me. Things happened that i don't understand. But it appears that everything that has occurred has happened for a reason.

Things happened during January 2001. The most profound thing that occurred was mentally with me. The relationship with You changed. Moreover, i believe things changed for me, more than for You. You have always been clear about our relationship. Now i understand.

Right now i'm sitting in the airport about to fly back to Atlanta. i already have begun to think of my next trip up. It's no longer a long drive up to be with You. The sad fact appears that although i want to be at home, I also want to be here with You and my brothers.

February 2000 – Initial contact thru IM and E-mails.

March 2000 – First but not the last visit

April 2000 – i signed my first contract

May 2000 – For the first time in several years, i attend IML as part of a Family.

June 2000 – Again, we attend SELF as a Leather Family.

July 2000 – We, as a Leather Family, went to watch the fireworks as the US celebrated the re-opening of the Washington Monument. During this same time, i began to suffer extremely high fevers from unknown causes. i don't remember the night it happened, but i know i had a fever of 103 and You took me to the Emergency Room. i didn't understand at that time why You would do that. In my mind, i should have been taking care of You. But as You have shown me, this relationship is a two-way street. Just as i love, respect, and care for You, You love, care, and respect me.

August 2000 – I'm still suffering from the fevers even after a lot of the tests. You are still there, giving me encouragement and love. Caring for me when i was sick.

September 2000 – We attend Olympia together as a Family. You allowed me to experience things that i never thought i would ever do.

October 2000 – This was a month to celebrate. Not only is it my birthday but Yours as well. You made me very happy when you unwrapped my present to you and read what it said. i saw tears in your eyes and i knew that i had gotten you the most perfect gift. my heart was happy!

Not only did we celebrate birthdays, but because of our relationship, i was afforded the chance of meeting someone who was to become my best friend but also become my leather brother. We shared a drive in the mountains, a trip to view the leaves.

November 2000 — With Your approval, i presented to the public myself, who am very shy, to help raise funds for MAsT.

December 2000 - i was with You just before Christmas. You decided to allow your three boys to go to Fort Lauderdale without You, so we three boys could have some time to bond and have a good time. This would also turn out to be the last time i would be the same boy as i was when i left on December 19.

January 2001 — Since i had seen You in December, something happened. i have since stopped searching for the reason why "it" happened. i'm content to know "it' happened for me and for You. my outlook on our relationship was changed. It changed withoutwords being exchanged, but thru actions and love. You sat beside me and held my hand in the hospital offering words of encouragement to speed me on my way to recovery. Once again, You were there for me. You allow one of my leather brothers, mike 2, to be there also. Having him there helped me, but i also think it helped him. The day i was released from the hospital, i asked for your help in washing my back because i simply had run out of energy. You did and never backed away, you were there for me andprovided me with love.

February 2001 - the recovery process is a long and very slow road. You still stood strong for me, and you never let me give up.

*****

Exactly, one month after slave tommy's death, I sat down and wrote him a letter of farewell and appreciation:

Farewell

My dear slave tommy,

I am writing this exactly one month after you left us. It has been quite a month. your memories are everywhere. I knew we were going to lose you but did not know when. I thought I was prepared, but I wasn't.

you left sooner than we expected, boy. And you left many memories in our hearts. Today, I want to give you thanks.

- Thanks, tommy, for being yourself.

- Thanks, tommy, for all your love.

- Thanks, tommy, for wearing your collar with so much pride.

- Thanks, tommy, for understanding what our family was all about.

- Thanks, tommy, for your constant smile.

- Thanks, tommy, for being there for your Master.

- Thanks, tommy, for being there for your brothers.

- Thanks, tommy, for your service.

- Thanks, tommy, for your loyalty.

- Thanks, tommy, for your courageous fight even that many times you felt "sick of getting sick."

- Thanks, tommy, for the opportunity of being part of your life.

- Thanks, tommy, for loving this Master the special way you did.

Being at your bed side with dave and mike was one of the most powerful and overwhelming experience of my lifetime. Seeing you in pain was hard. But when you finally left, surrounded by those who love you, your mother, sister and brother, your Leather Family, and your brothers and sisters from your Lakota spirituality circle, I knew you left happy and full of love. I will never forget our last exchange of words, just minutes before your passing. "tommy, we love you" and you responded "love you too."

While being at your bedside to the moment of your last breath, I realized that the love that you, dave, mike and I were sharing at that moment is what makes this family strong... it's what this, our Leather Family, is all about.

During our stay with your family and friends, we were overwhelmed by their showing appreciation for helping you to have fun during the last year and a half of your life. They all knew how happy you were coming to DC and our family road trips. And with your passing, you left all of us as a strong family, you left us your Mom and siblings, you left us Laura, and Michael and Gen, who feel so strongly being part of us. What a gift you left us with at the very moment of your passing.

Then two weeks later, the friends you made through the Leather Family gathered in our home to remember and celebrate your life.you should have been happy looking down at us and seeing how many people really care for you. It was good to have your ashes back in the house, your last trip to the family's home.

tommy, you will always live in our hearts. There are memories of you in every single corner of our house, so your presence among us is always strong and vibrant. Still, we miss your smile and your ways. you were so unique and so special, boy. We do not have any other choice but to love you for what you were.

My last command to you as my slave is to accept my appointment as our Ambassador before the Almighty and the special Guardian Angel of each member of our family.

Daddy loves and misses you so much, boy.

Master Taíno

When a slave is in his Master's arms, he feels safe, protected and loved.
He feels he belongs.

Master Taíno

Slave Delivery

My slave Neil served me for two years, from 2001 to late 2003. Those were two great years, and I cherish that relationship, which included competing for the International Master/slave title in 2003.

When Neil was in my service, he continued to live in the Chelsea neighborhood of New York City. I had three other slaves at home, including a gay couple who served me together. However, Neil was my primary slave.

During that time he would come to Virginia on weekends, and I was a frequent visitor to New York to be with him. I enjoyed going to the Big Apple, as I also participated in events there. Hanging out and giving demos at The L.U.R.E. Leather bar, participating in MAsT meetings, going to the parties at the Bondage Club, and other kinky events.

We cared and loved each other a lot, but the relationship stalled, mostly due to the distance between us. I realized this before slave Neil but waited until he came to the same conclusion, which he did.

The interesting and remarkable occurrence happened when and how we ended our formal relationship. We agreed to do a private uncollaring ceremony in my dungeon, the same place he was collared two years earlier, with only the two of us. That ceremony was even more powerful and emotional than the collaring one had been, as we had developed a great affinity and love for each other, even though we were parting ways. I still remember that moment fondly.

Slave Neil asked me to remain as his Guardian Master in a role to protect him and vet any new potential Master. I accepted this with delight. I believe this is a great testament to our relationship. There was never an ounce of hard feelings by either of us.

A year later he called me to let me know he was talking to a Master in Chicago. I made a call to a well-known Master and friend in the Windy City, and he confirmed the credentials and character of Neil's prospective Master. He also let me know that the Master was physically handicapped and eventually would be confined to a wheelchair. When I passed the information on to Neil, he replied that he knew this, and that was one of the reasons he wanted to serve him. This reflects the character and heart of my former slave.

Months later Neil was ready to move to Chicago with his new Master. He called me one day to ask me for a favor. He was a board member of GMSMA, a very well-known gay BDSM group in New York. The Board was going to throw a farewell party for him before he left for Chicago, and Neil wanted me to be there. I happily agreed. I told Neil I thought he was going to ask me to take him to Chicago to his new Master, as I owned a conversion van.

"Would you?" he asked.

Of course I would. I cared deeply for the boy. He did not own a vehicle, and I knew that the logistics to move would be very challenging and costly for him. It was going to be a pleasure to help him.

When the day came, I drove to New York City with my new slave to pick up Neil and all the stuff that he would take with him. He gifted me several things that he would not need at his new Master's place, including his silverware set. I love that set and have used it at home in DC for years. Now the set resides in my apartment in Costa Rica. Those forks and knives often bring good memories of my time with slave Neil.

We drove over 14 hours from Chelsea to Chicago. We arrived in the evening to his new Master's house, and I literally delivered my former slave to his new Master. Some people did not understand why I did that. Simple! I was more than happy to do it. It was part of my responsibility as his Guardian Master. It was also due to the caring nature of our relationship.

At the time, Rick Storer, then Executive Director of the Leather Archives & Museum, told me that he had never seen any Master taking his former slave to a new Master. I did, and I am very glad I did so. They have been together for almost two decades now, which makes me so happy for both.

Leather is not what
you wear...
Leather is a way of
living...
Leather should be
in your heart.

Master Taino

Butchmanns Academy

Master Steve, the man I consider my mentor, invited me to his Butchmanns BDSM Academy. That was in February of 2002, after he had relocated from Palm Springs to Tucson, Arizona. He asked me to be a guest instructor. I asked him why he wanted me, as I was still early on in my own Mastery journey. His answer was, as I was to come to know, typical of him.

"Just bring your heart," he said.

I did bring my heart, and also brought my hunger, interest, and desire to learn more. After all, I had only just started my own academy four months before.

After flying from DC to Tucson, which included a seven-hour wait sitting on two different planes in Dallas, Texas, due to a rare snowstorm, I finally landed that evening at Tucson Airport.

Master Steve's slave picked me up at the airport and greeted me by presenting on his knees and telling me that his Master honored me. I was so surprised to see him acting so openly by presenting right in the middle of a busy airport. It was the first learning lesson of a busy week at Butchmanns.

I arrived three days early to allow time for me to become familiar with Master Steve's household, protocols, and the preparations for the weekend event. I cherish the fact that I had plenty of time for talking with Master Steve. Well, mostly listening to his wisdom, as I began to respect him even more. My then slave Neil arrived from New York the following day and joined me for the rest of the week.

When Friday arrived, the awesome complex grew very busy. Teachers like Master Skip and SlaveMaster led the faculty with Master Steve. They were known as the "Three

Amigos." Masters and slaves both arrived that weekend as students attending the Academy.

This was the first Butchmanns event taking place in their new facilities, which had been built next to Master Steve's home. The building included a huge dormitory with metal bunk beds and a couple of regular rooms, plus a gym-sized dungeon or play space that was amazing. Among the things that I noticed and used myself once I returned home, were the black metal bunks for slaves to sleep in, and the stainless-steel bowls used by the slaves to eat in. When I got back home, I bought three sets of similar bunks, as well as bowls that were to be used by the slaves who attended our academy.

Butchmanns program was based on the BDSM practices of cathartic flogging, mumification, and piercing, plus spirituality and the Master/slave dynamic.

I was more experienced in the cathartic flogging segment. After addressing what flogging was all about, Master Steve allowed everyone to experience a flogging, either giving or receiving. Submissives/slaves were told to ask any of the Dominants/Masters to flog them. Meanwhile, the dominants attending also had an opportunity to learn and practice their flogging techniques.

As soon as Master Steve gave the go-ahead to begin, a handsome slave came directly to me and requested to be flogged. He was a gay slave from New England and was in attendance with his partner, who was learning the art of Mastery. I try never to begin a flogging with any predetermined expectations; I always go with the flow. Whatever happens, happens.

I am comfortable with whatever the submissive/slave gives me during the experience. This slave needed a good intense flogging, and the experience was amazing and very powerful for him. The flogging took him into a very profound catharsis. Afterward, he began a constant stream of sobbing and crying out of control. Eventually, while still holding the boy, I looked to my slave Neil, and he figured out that I wanted him to get the boy's Master. His Master, who was practicing flogging on the other side of the huge dungeon, came and assisted me with his aftercare.

This is something I have done often when I am flogging someone else's property in the presence of his or her owner, and when I have flogged Masters or Dominants in the presence of their slaves or submissives. A couple of years later, during a visit to DC, the boy asked to visit me at my house for a repeat, and I was very happy to do so. According to him, I have been the only one to take him where he needs to go when being flogged.

Later that afternoon, another participant, this time a young man from South America, asked for a flogging. He was an extremely built guy with a very wide back, which provided an excellent canvas for flogging. He also was able to tolerate and enjoy an intense pounding by my floggers.

Afterwards, toward the end of his aftercare, I said I believed that he was still flying.

"Yes Sir, flying First Class," he responded, and I just laughed.

He went on to comment that this high was better than any achieved using chemical substances.

Because I have never used drugs, his remark provided a learning lesson for me. The natural endorphin rush or high that a flogging produces is like the feeling induced by other, more tangible substances.

My slave Neil was also transported to an emotional and mental high during our hot wax play. In this scenario, I continually poured hot paraffin onto his shaved body, over and over again.

That weekend I made many new friends and solidified friendships with other kinksters. Some of those friendships are still going strong today, more than two decades later.

I assisted in teaching, but I also learned a lot that weekend. I came back with some great memories and experiences. I am thankful Master Steve gave me that opportunity, because it was one of the best weekends I've experienced during my long journey into self-discovery.

Forcing Catharsis

Early in my journey a disgruntled person accused me of forcing catharsis on people I flog. I do not believe catharsis should be forced. However, I do guide the participant who has requested it into experiencing catharsis when I flog. I experienced a cathartic flogging myself early in my journey and was transformed by it. I have a very high rate of success in taking people into catharsis through flogging, and I have also halted a session several times when I realized at the time it was not right for them and was not going to happen.

A couple of decades ago I did force an individual into accepting a cathartic experience even though he thought he wouldn't get there. Bill was an older gentleman with a lot of BDSM experience, but he felt he had been used as a whipping post or as an object, because he could endure heavy intensity during impact play. He had never felt that connection between giver and receiver.

This happened during the first year of the MTTA Academy. When the Cathartic Flogging class ended, and all participants were given the opportunity to experience it, Bill accepted but warned me that he would not go for the emotional catharsis. I decided to do my work and take him where he truly needed to go.

I did this for two reasons. First, I knew his story, as I had met him and seen him playing in New York City before he attended the Academy. He needed to have a loving, caring, cathartic experience in order to let go of the pain accumulated throughout his life.

Second, I knew intensity was not an issue for him, and I would be able to push just the right amount that would allow him to reach catharsis.

I flogged him long and hard. It was very intense. We did not stop until he relinquished his pain in a much-needed explosive catharsis. Yes, I pushed him into experiencing what he needed, but I did not break his trust nor was I asked to stop.

Bill has given permission, allowing me to use part of his end-of-Academy evaluation to be included with his name and story:

> The moment of truth came for me late Saturday night/early Sunday morning in the dungeon when Master Taíno flogged me. My brothers and slave neil honored me with their presence. i wanted to look good for the family. i wanted to take whatever Master Taíno wanted to give me. i wanted to fly. But i did not expect to have my life turned around. Thank You SIR for not giving up, for holding me afterward and loving me while i, even then, fought unsuccessfully not to cry. i have found a new focus for my sensual/sexual/life energies. i am not the same as when i arrived at Your house last Friday. Thank You for taking a chance with me, for knowing where i needed to go and taking me there.

I knew Bill was going to be alright. My reward came more than a decade later, when we ran into each other at the memorial for slave David Stein in New York City. I told him that I often use his story in my Cathartic Flogging class as an example of the only instance when I did consensually force a person to find his cathartic moment; although at that time I never mentioned his name.

"Master Taíno, you can use my name. You changed my life that day, and I am grateful for that," he told me while we hugged.

Men Don't Cry

A year after my slave tommy died, I returned to Atlanta for his Memorial and the spreading of his ashes in the Lakota circle within the confines of his backyard.

On the eve of the Memorial, I went to the Atlanta Eagle, where I met a gorgeous young man. This young man seemed to follow me everywhere I went, and I perceived that he'd like to be flogged by me. I decided to approach him and ask if he'd like to be flogged. He did welcome the idea.

I did not want to take him to a catharsis state in a public venue, but it was too late! When I was taking the restraints off him, he started to sob and cry. I immediately embraced him tenderly, administering aftercare.

The boy became livid and very angry. I figured out quickly what was wrong. He was not happy that he was crying, especially in public. He confessed that he was raised that men do not cry, ever. That was the wrong thing to do to him as a child, in my opinion.

He wanted to leave the bar. I tried to hold him gently and explain to him that it was okay, but eventually, he walked out of the bar. I was the person who took him to that cathartic state, so he was my responsibility. I followed him to his car. He opened the car doors and I got into the passenger seat. After a bit, we started talking. He kept repeating how wrong it was for him to cry in public.

I wanted to convince this young man that it was okay to express his emotions after receiving a cathartic flogging. I had an idea.

"What do you think about me?" I asked him.

He responded that I was a Master: I was strong, a dominant person, and so on.

"What will you think when I tell you that tomorrow at 5:25 p.m., I am going to be crying and expressing my emotions, openly and in public?" I replied.

He couldn't believe what I was saying. I explained, telling him that I came to Atlanta that weekend for the Memorial of my slave. The next day, Sunday, at 5:25 p.m., would be the exact time that my slave passed away the year before. His mother agreed for me to speak at the Memorial at that exact time in honor of my beloved slave. I knew I would not be able to control my emotions and I would cry and probably sob with grief.

Because I was being honest and presented myself as vulnerable and accepting of my own emotions, he listened and absorbed my message. That did it for him. We returned to the Eagle and eventually to his apartment to end the evening.

Years later he ran into me online, and we talked about the experience. He was surprised that I told him the exact day of our encounter, and I had to remind him why I was in Atlanta that weekend.

His father and society had taught him that men do not cry. This Master taught him differently that evening. Men can and should cry, as it is normal and very healthy.

Dance of Souls

During the second Southwest Leather Conference held in Phoenix, Arizona, December of 2003, I was invited to present and be a judge for the Southwest Master/slave contest. This was the first time this event had taken place within a hotel.

The event became a learning experience for me, particularly due to the Dance of Souls on Sunday afternoon. This was something completely new for me. Men and women getting pierced and dancing to the sound of drums — a very evocative ritual with Native American origins. Because the event was still small at that time, the Dance of Souls consisted of two big rings with about ten people pierced, with ropes attached to each of the rings. Everyone danced around the ring, while also moving around the ballroom. Each participant had an unpierced dancer supporting them.

This was very new to me, but fascinating as well. I sat down and carefully observed what was happening. There was something very powerful happening in the room. There was such good energy flowing. I must admit that at the time I did not realize the importance and significance of energy as I do now. But that Sunday afternoon I learned and felt a lot.

This was my first time in Phoenix, and I did not know very many people. Most of the people pierced for the Dance were unknown to me personally, although I had seen them throughout the weekend event. I kept watching everything that was happening. I was hungry to learn and explore this new experience that the kink community was offering me.

Most people were already pierced and had joined the others in the two rings. It was then I noticed a young, straight boy that I had been introduced to at the beginning of the weekend, getting pierced. After the piercing was complete, he jumped into the center of the ballroom full of energy and joined the ring. He was being assisted by a big guy who started dancing, supporting him. He was a good-looking boy and so full of energy that he pulled my attention back to him repeatedly. He was fun to watch and to witness how he was completely immersed in the ritual.

The Dance of Souls was a completely new experience for me, and the energy that was flowing was incredible. However, I was not ready for what happened next.

While they were moving and dancing around the ballroom, the boy and his supporter kept getting close to where I was sitting and watching. Suddenly, the guy who was supporting the boy left and disappeared. I stood up in disbelief. My understanding was that every pierced participant needed a dancer supporting them, and now the boy was alone. Not sure why, even to this day, I jumped into the dancing area and joined the boy to support him. I have never done anything like that in my life. But I did enjoy it and continued all the way, until it was over. I accompanied him until his hooks were removed from his chest. It was a powerful experience, serious and fun, and extremely spiritual as well.

Right after the Dance of Souls, I ran into the guy who was supporting the boy and asked him why he had left him alone. His answer overwhelmed me. He said that he felt the energy flowing between me and the boy, so when they were closer to me, he left so I could join the boy. To this day I am not sure I understand how he could feel that I was connected to the boy during the event.

This personal experience at my first Dance of Souls was part of my continuous and evolving journey; this time learning more about the power of energy. I continued to attend and participate in the Dance of Souls at SWLC for many years thereafter. It has brought more positive energy and spirituality to my Leather journey.

I have become a firm believer in energy. During my BDSM practice, I have learned that I am transmitting my energy to those I play with — usually during impact play. I now convert my play into spiritual experiences, in particular with my floggers, which is how I learned to bring my play partners to catharsis.

It is important to remember those who have shown us the way and have influenced our journey in positive ways. I shall not forget my mentors and guides.

Master Taino

Berlin Airport Service

During Holy Week in Berlin, Germany, the famous Leather Week Event takes place as well, with kinky parties by the dozen happening each day of the week. In 2005 I was able to attend this wonderful kink debauchery. I had amazing fun every single day. But what happened at the Berlin Airport leaving Germany for Madrid, Spain, is what really made for a fantastic and ever-lasting story and memory.

At the Berlin Airport there is security at every gate instead of in the main terminal. When called to board we had to pass through security, as expected. As this was post 9/11, I had to remove my boots. After I was cleared by Security, a man approached me and offered to help me with my boots. I was so surprised that I declined. I decided to sit and put all my stuff back together, and as I bent down to put on my boots, there he was kneeling in front of me, ready to help me with my boots. I was very surprised, but this time I obliged and allowed him to assist me with the boots.

When he finished, he introduced himself and said that he knew who I was through the internet, he knew I was in Berlin for Leather Week, and he wanted to meet me so badly. Unfortunately, it did not happen as we traversed the dozens of parties held during the week. So, when he realized we were on the same flight to Madrid, he did not hesitate to jump at the chance to serve me anyway he could.

We boarded our flight to Madrid, and he sat several rows behind me. During the flight I began to plan for my arrival at the Madrid Barajas Airport. I have been to Madrid before and liked its Metro system. I knew the cheapest way to get to my hostel in the gay neighborhood of Chueca was by train.

On a trip to the restroom, I stopped by the Leather boy's seat and asked him if he was taking the train to downtown Madrid. He replied he was not, as he had to catch a connection to the Basque Country where he lived. However, without hesitation he asked what I needed. His lay-over at the airport was a long one, so he volunteered to assist me — another opportunity to serve this Master.

After landing at Barajas, he carried my luggage and invited me for coffee and croissants. There, we had a chance to talk and get to know each other. Shortly afterward, he went to get the information on how to catch the Metro to Chueca. He found out that I needed to take a bus to the other terminal where the Metro station was. He carried my luggage all the way to the bus, where we had to say our good-byes.

I was fascinated with his personal story. His need and desire to serve me, whom he had been reading about for some time on the Internet. I was very impressed when he jumped at the opportunity to serve me publicly at the Berlin Airport. I thought I would never see him again, although I would never forget his deep desire to serve me.

Thankfully, I was wrong! I returned to Madrid eight years later, and I ran into him again at a BDSM play party. I cannot remember if I flogged him at the party, but most likely I did.

The Kilt

As early as I can remember I have been a part of Gay Leather culture, as it was the epitome of masculinity in our community. Personally, although I believe everyone's kinks are their own, for myself I have never been fond of things like cross-dressing or feminine clothing on men. When I began to see Leathermen in kilts, I was shocked and jokingly referred to the kilts as *skirts*.

Around 2005, I told my good friend Master Skip that I believed kilts were just *skirts* while he was wearing a kilt. He warned me that one day he would make me wear a kilt, and I just laughed it off. Later I learned that teasing Master Skip was a big mistake.

A few months after that encounter, I was on stage during MsC 2005 when Master Skip was called to the stage. I knew that this was not part of the script. My friend began telling the crowd about my disdain for kilts.

While he was doing that, a group of fellow Masters began to walk onto the stage and made a circle around me. True to his warning, they had purchased a kilt from one of the MsC vendors and proceeded to put it around my waist over my leather pants. I took it as a joke and a good moment among friends. The kilt came home with me and ended up in my closet. I did not have any intention to wear it. Bad omen.

Somehow the following year, the kilt found its way to MsC 2006. Once again, Master Skip challenged me on stage to wear the kilt the way it is supposed to be worn, with nothing underneath. He promised to raise money for the MsC titleholders' travel fund if I would do so. As I am committed to our event as well as to our titleholders, I agreed to do it.

In a matter of minutes, over a thousand dollars were raised from the audience wanting to see me, Master Taíno, wearing a kilt. I had no choice but to go backstage, take off my leather pants, and put the kilt on.

The story does not end there, however! Everyone began to praise me for wearing the kilt and commenting on the good shape of my legs, a product of a lot of bicycling as a child. So I started wearing the darn kilt at some events and other specific situations.

My favorite time to wear my kilt has been during the Dance of Souls at the Southwest Leather Conference in Phoenix, AZ. At this sacred event, I love to wear my kilt and nothing else, while dancing to the sound of the drums.

Sadly, over a decade later, my gift from Master Skip no longer fit. Upon hearing this, dear friend slave raven, who was emceeing MsC, gifted me a larger one, which I still have and wear. After that, I gifted the original kilt to Jota, a young member of my leather family from Costa Rica.

The kilt became just another symbol of my continuing evolution. I progressed from despising kilts to now wearing mine without any issue, thanks to my dear friend, Master Skip.

Trans boy

In June of 2006, I traveled to New York City to attend the traditional Leather Pride Night and Folsom Fair East, as I used to do every year. During LPN I ran into a 21-year-old, cute, short college student. He was adorable, and I reached out to him. We hit it off well — we connected great and were having fun. His name was Brandon.

Taking care of my always ailing back, I ended up sitting down on a sofa and had the boy kneeling on the floor before me, while we continued engaging with each other.

As usual, I was touching him all over, and all of a sudden I realized I was touching . . . a binder. A binder is what pre-op trans men use to flatten their breasts. At that moment I realized that Brandon was an FTM, a female to male trans man. Immediately I told myself, "So, what? I see a boy. He is cute and adorable. We are connecting well, we are sharing great energy, and everything is good."

I continued enjoying the boy without telling him what I had discovered. About half an hour later I tried to pull off his shirt, and Brandon, a bit scared, told me there was something he needed to tell me.

"I am a FTM trans man," he said.

"Oh, I know," I replied.

His face held so much relief. I will never forget it. He realized that I was accepting him as a man, as a sub boy, as a human being.

"I'm tired of being rejected," he immediately added.

He also shared that he chose his name to honor Brandon Teena, a trans boy who was raped and murdered by two guys in Nebraska.

Next day we spent time at the Fair. A couple of months later Brandon was visiting me in DC and attending MsC as my guest. We have been friends ever since, and my slave Paul adores him.

This story was an important part of my journey. I consider that split second when I realized Brandon was a trans boy to be one of the most powerful moments in my life.

Lesson learned? I learned that day that it's perfectly okay to be intimate with a trans boy; that I can connect and have fun as with any other young man. Since then I have connected without any hesitation with many other trans boys.

If Brandon had contacted me online and let me know that he was trans and wanted to meet me, I would have had to analyze what to do and how to deal with it. Thankfully, it happened while I had already connected with him as a human being. Years later, I considered a different trans boy to join my household as a slave.

Photo Courtesy of Judith Oppenheimer

I was outraged, though, that such a wonderful human being at age twenty-one was already tired of being rejected and discriminated against by gay men. What a shame!

Since that incident I have been outspoken denouncing people that merely give lip service to trans individuals while avoiding developing relationships or engaging in intimacy with them.

This story ranks very high in my journey.

We will be a much better community when we learn to welcome and celebrate our diversity.

Master Taíno

The Lion Will Never Sleep Again

In 2008, I was invited to present some classes during SINSations in Leather, a kinky event taking place in Chicago. The event had booked the entire hotel, which made for an amazing weekend of fun, kink, BDSM, and debauchery in total privacy.

This event was a pansexual event, which meant that most attendees were straight. I have attended many pansexual events along my journey. As a gay man, the issue for me personally has been that most of the attendees that are also gay men tend to be coupled or not the type of men that I prefer. That was the case at SINSations as well.

However, during this event, a mutual lady friend introduced me to Will, a very attractive, tall, gay young man. Immediately I knew I wanted to play with him; specifically, I wanted to flog him. He expressed his interest, even though he identified mostly as a top and dominant.

We agreed to play that night in the ballroom, which was converted into a large dungeon for the event. He warned me that he may have wild reactions and may even turn a bit aggressive at the end of the session. I was glad he warned me, although I did not change my mind and still wanted to play with him.

We had an amazing session. His reactions were loud — his face so expressive that many people stopped their scenes to watch us. What made this a special story was the end and aftercare, and more importantly, how very much his life itself was impacted.

After we had finished and as he had warned me, he did turn very aggressive towards me after I removed the restraints. He was bigger and taller than I, so I grabbed him and took him down to the floor, where I embraced him firmly and as tightly as I could. I ended up providing aftercare on the floor, while dozens of attendees watched from all around us.

Will ended up attending our Master/slave Conference a year later. When I reached out to him to request his permission to use his name in his story in this book, he let me know how MsC and I had influenced him.

After this experience, Will sent me one of the most powerful letters I have ever received. He succinctly detailed his flogging experience and the impact it had had in his life. At that time, he gave me permission to use it for my Cathartic Flogging classes. As I have said so many times before, there is no better reward than for one human being to be able to make a positive difference in another human being's life.

Here is Will's letter:

Dear Master Taíno,

You asked me to write to you about the experience we shared at SINSations in Leather in Chicago.

At that event, you became the second person who had ever flogged me, and the first time I had ever completely surrendered my mind and body to a BDSM experience.

To fully explain what this meant to me, I have to tell you this: I grew up in an unhappy home, where I was rejected by my parents if I too strenuously expressed my needs and desires.

I learned from the moment I was born that expressing my personal power would result in abandonment.

As an adult, I have been blessed with a great capacity to express tenderness, sincerity, and love, but have often felt like half a man, because I have been fearful to experience "power emotions" — aggressiveness, strength, and anger.

I expected my first flogging would be merely a surrender of my body to the control of another person.

I expected that taking the scene "all the way" meant that my spirit would be broken, and that I would collapse at the conclusion, as I had witnessed so often in other scenes, in a crying, sobbing heap, clinging to the boots of my Top as my only connection back to the "real world."

However, rather than my spirit being broken, it was released.

The true surrender for me was a surrender to an exchange of power that I can only describe as spiritual.

As you poured your physical, mental (and I hope, sexual) energy into my flesh, bones, and blood, the part of my nature that I had been taught to suppress all my life came tearing out of my soul.

During our experience I recall roaring and growling and feeling more powerful and alive than I have ever felt.

I would never have thought that in allowing myself to be powerless — to be restrained and beaten — that my fear of my own power would be stripped away, that the lion in my heart would be awakened and come roaring to the surface.

In the week since our experience I have already noticed a change in my thinking, my stance, my outlook on life.

I have taken a great leap toward becoming the man I was meant to be. The lion will never sleep again. This was your gift to me.

Of all the things I could thank you for, the one thing that I'll never forget is the control, wisdom, and grace you displayed at the end of our scene. When I rushed at you, you knew exactly what was happening, and you allowed me to experience it and eventually embraced me for it.

Unlike my parents, you did not abandon me in that life-changing moment.

Thank you, Master Taíno, from my heart.

With tenderness and respect,

Will

St. Louis, Missouri

Slave Paul

During my journey, I have had numerous slaves, many of them for only a short period of time. Sometimes others wonder why I have slaves for just a couple of years. The main reason is my deep attraction to young men. I welcome into my life young men new to BDSM and M/s relationships, I teach them as much as they wish to absorb, and then let them fly. I am extremely proud that several of my former slaves are now in very long-term relationships with their respective Masters and that they credit what they learned from me for their success. The two slaves with the longest time of service have been slave David, for nine years, from 2005 to his tragic death in 2014, and slave Paul from 2010 to the present.

I have created a process for potential slaves, no matter whether I met them in a Leather Bar, at organized events, or online. Each one must complete a comprehensive application and an interview, followed by in-home visits.

However, my current slave Paul did not follow that process. I jokingly say that he entered my life and my house through the kitchen door, where he promptly took over the kitchen. I met slave Paul in 2005, during his first attendance at MsC, when he still lived in Maine. Years later he moved with his family to Northern Virginia, a few miles south of my home. He was also working in my neighborhood.

One day in early 2010, he showed up at my house after being referred to me by a dear slave friend of his. He asked me if he could enter my service as a way for him to be able to serve the community. He was clear that he did not want to be my slave. He had been collared several times, very unsuccessfully, and did not want to go through the same experience again.

I knew slave Paul was a great slave, although he was not the type of slave that I usually searched for. But, as he did not want to be a slave, that scenario was not an issue. I did clarify with him from day one that sex was not going to be part of our dynamic. Each time that I have had a slave that I will not be sexually attracted to, I let them know from the start that sex is not included in their service. That is why I always reiterate that sex and BDSM are not required for a M/s relationship. What it is required is the surrender of the slave and the Master assuming responsibility for him.

I did accept slave Paul's petition. His request coincided with my decision to open my Leather Family to others who were not slaves within my household, and I also decided to integrate Sir Ross, a young straight Dominant from New York City that I was mentoring, into the family. I got the sense that slave Paul needed a place to belong. While accepting him into my service, I invited him to the Leather Family. He welcomed the idea and accepted and began to come to the house to help around.

By March, 2010, he had attended the MTTA Academy, which cemented his path as a slave, and became immersed in the programs of MTTA as a staff member.

Then in May of 2010, Sir Ross and slave Paul were inducted into the Family during a small ceremony that took place in our home on a Sunday afternoon.

Shortly after, he asked if he could move to the house to serve me more directly alongside the rest of my slaves. I welcomed him into my home, where he had an even better opportunity to display his skills in the kitchen, as a handyman, gardener, and a man of all trades.

Even after living in my home, Paul still did not want to become my slave. We talked about it several times. I continually assured him by guaranteeing that nothing would change after I collared him and made him my slave. That was his issue, as each time he agreed to be collared, things immediately changed. I decided that I would give him all the time he needed, and if he ever decided he wanted to be my slave, I would accept him.

Finally on August 30, 2010, he wrote me his petition, which I have included at the end of this story. Paul was officially collared as my slave in October of 2010.

slave Paul has become not only the longest a slave has ever served me, but he has also become instrumental in our home and with my educational goals concerning MTTA. He immersed himself by working with both the Academy and the Master/slave Conference. As both programs grew and got more complicated, he became my right hand and my partner in running them. He did this with so much gusto, with so much passion, and with so much joy. I have said publicly many times that I would not have been able to produce MsC this last decade without him at my side taking care of so many things I could not.

slave Paul fulfilled his goal to serve the Community at the same time he served me, while he was also able to convince himself that he could have and serve a Master who values his service.

Here is his petition from August 30, 2010, which also tells his side of the story.

> Master,
>
> Over my travels I have used a meditation called "The Sacrament of Letting Go." It talks of loss, waiting, growing, and finally rebirth. It talks of a tree that every year must die to survive the winter only to be reborn in the spring . . . renewed in the light and nutrients given from its protector. This meditation has become my life story.

For seven years I've searched for something in my life. That "something" has evaded me and caused me to not only search outward but inward also. Over the past couple of months, I have come to realize what that "something" really is . . . my slaveheart, the core of who I am.

My journey to this moment has not been easy. There has been a lot of hurt and inadvertently hurting of others, only to prove that the lesson for me was a life lesson . . . good or bad, but one that needed to be taught. The hard times have taught me what I don't want, and the good what I do want. It has taught me where I need to grow and what is important in my life and what I just need to put away.

Along with the lows come the highs of learning who I am and what I can accomplish when I set my mind to it. I've learned how to effectively deal with problems but most importantly what slavery really means to me and how it affects my everyday living.

Master, throughout my journey I've seen you standing there. On my first journey to the Master/slave conference I met you... having been told exactly who you were and being a newbie slave, I was scared to death . . . someone as unprepared as myself meeting someone of the stature as yourself . . . what was I thinking? But you hugged me and welcomed me to the fold nonetheless. The following year when I returned to the conference not only did you welcome me back but welcomed me back by name . . . my heart knew it was home back then. Every year since, I have grown closer to you and to all that you stand for.

On May 29th, 2010, you accepted me as part of your Leather family. That day will always have a special place in my heart. For the first time on this journey, I am part of a loving, giving family that accepts who I am and where I am in my life. My heart and life became united and complete once again.

Master, as I look to the future, I see no better place to study and learn than under a Master who is viewed as a pillar of the community. Slave wen has always told me that when the student is ready the teacher will be there. How right she was.

Master, I have served you for the past four months with all my heart, soul, love, and devotion. I can give you only one more thing . . . the key to your slave's collar . . . Master, I formally petition for a full collar in your household as a slave to you.

I fully understand what this means to me and to the family dynamic. I also understand that before this can become your will there need to be many discussions with everyone involved. When you are ready for that, please let me know.

Until that time, I remain,

In service and Leather,

slave paul

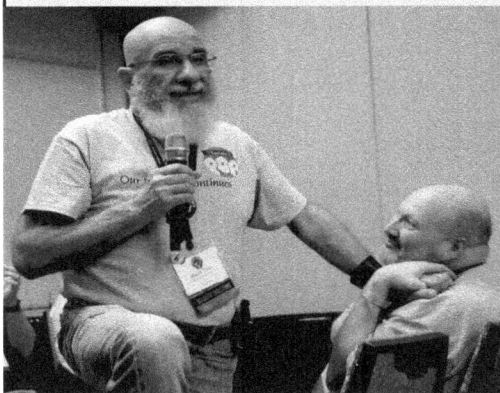

Photo Courtesy of Kathryn Madarasz

Everyone should take the responsibility for teaching and mentoring the younger folks as they are the future of our Kinky Community.

Master Taino

Early Journey

Master Taíno (Early 90s)

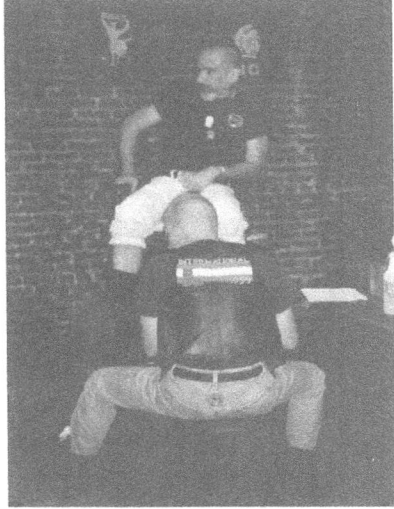

Master Taíno with Bob Ehrlich
International Boot Black 1999
(2000)

Master Taíno (2001)

Master Taíno at
Capital Pride March

Leather Family

Leather Family at MsC 2023
Photo Courtesy of Efraín González

Master Taíno with his four boys at Olympia (2002)

Master Taíno with slaves Paul, David and Mordecai (2013)
Photo Courtesy of Yali Molina

Master Taíno with Gypsie
Photo Courtesy of Bob Rubel

Master Taíno with Master J
Photo Courtesy of Bob Rubel

Master Taíno with Master Robert
Photo Courtesy of Bob Rubel

Master Taíno walking slave Jenna down the aisle during her wedding (2013)
Photo Courtesy of Bob Rubel

Folsom Street Fair (San Francisco)

Hot Red Back

An expression of happiness and fulfillment

His first flogging ever at the Mr S Booth

Intense paddling and flogging

Flogging a beautiful Asian boy

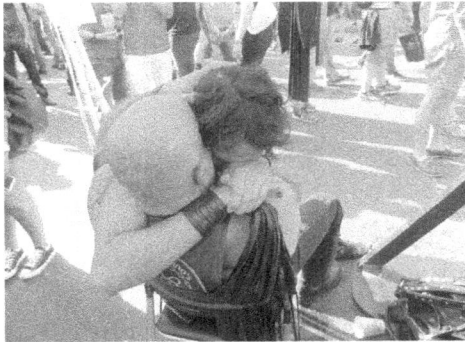
A deep catharsis required good aftercare

His face says it all

Aftercare for a handsome boy

Folsom Street East (New York City)

A good flogging
and spanking

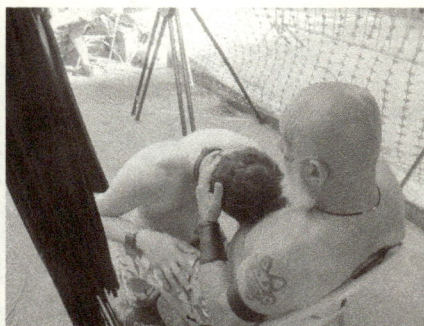

Kneeling in appreciation
before the Master

Caring for a boy after a flogging

Happy boy showing off his red back and butt

A kiss on the back after the flogging

A handsome boy had the experience of his life

Yes, I care a lot for this boy

This boy enjoyed his flogging

Leather Friends

Master Taíno with his Leather
sister, Lady Lynette
Photo Courtesy of Michael Riley

Master Taíno with his
Leather brother,
Master David
Photo Courtesy of Sir Roberto

Master Taíno embraces
Mister Blue and BlueFrost
when they won the
International M/s 2018 title
*Photo Courtesy of Hromovy
Drakzena*

Master Taíno
with Master Alex
Keppeler, former
Executive Director of
MAsT International
*Photo Courtesy of
Bob Rubel*

Master Taíno with
Mama Vi Johnson

Master Taíno with
Argentinian writer
Pablo Pérez

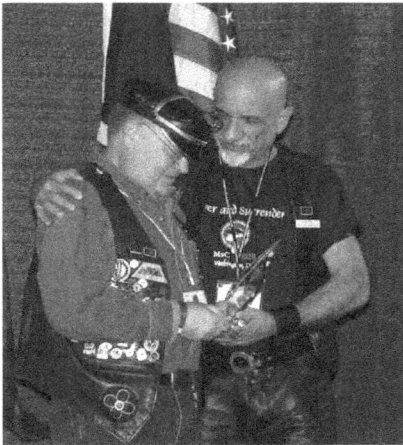

Master Taíno with Master
Tip from New York City
Photo Courtesy of Bob Rubel

Master Taíno with
Ms Diana
Photo Courtesy of
Kathryn Madarasz

Master/slave Conference (MsC)

Master Taíno receiving
a recognition from the
producers of MAsT '99 (2009)
Photo Courtesy of Bob Rubel

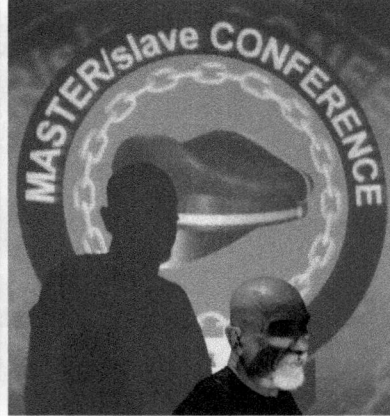

An amazing photo of Master
Taíno with his shadow and
the MsC Logo (2010)
Photo Courtesy of Mz Max Rulz

Lady Lynette
and Sir Stephen,
long time
MsC Associate
Producers (2014)
*Photo Courtesy of
Michael Riley*

Master Taíno with
the late slave David stein (2016)

Master Taíno with Master
Skip and slave Rick (2017)
*Photo Courtesy of
Shaan Michael Wade*

Master Taíno after
announcing his retirement
as MsC Producer in 2022
and passing the torch to
Mister Blue
*Photo Courtesy of Efrain
Gonzalez)*

Guy Baldwin presenting
the Guy Baldwin Master/
slave Heritage Award
2019 to Master Taíno
*Photo Courtesy of Kathryn
Madarasz*

Master Taíno with
Sir Stephen, MsC
Associate Producer
*Photo Courtesy of
Michael Riley*

Costa Rica

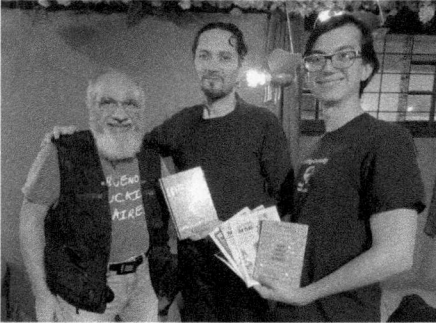

Master Taíno with Master Kai and Jota at a MAsT San José meeting

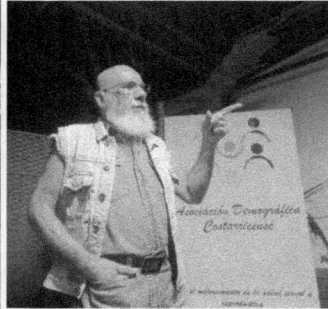

Offering a BDSM M/s class at Asociación Demográfica Costarricense in 2019

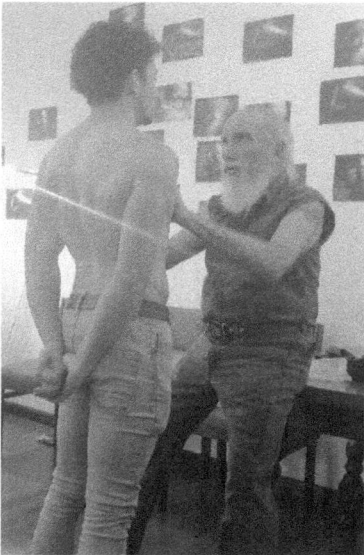

A BDSM class at Masculinidades Diversas in 2020

Teaching about flogging

Being interviewed alongside Jota and
Master Kai for a podcast in 2023

Presenting before Psychology students at
the University of Costa Rica in 2021

During a MAsT San José meeting

Master Taíno with the three Costa
Rican members of his Leather Family:
Jota, Orc and M.

Master Taíno thru the lens of photographers

Photo Courtesy of Kevin

Photo Courtesy of Yali Molina

Photo Courtesy of Bob Rubel

Photo Courtesy of Mark Chester

Photo Courtesy of Mz. Max Rulz

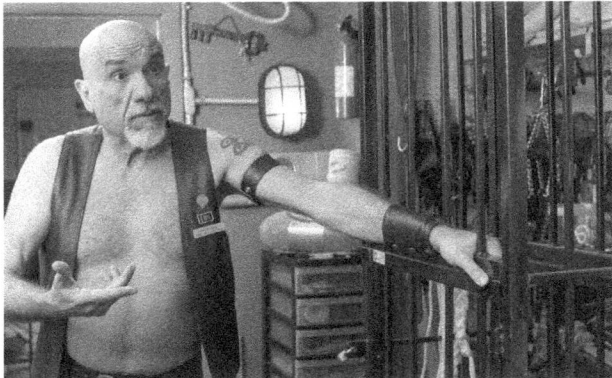

Photo Courtesy of Yali Molina

Slave Paul

Master Taíno and slave Paul at the Stonewall Inn in New York City

Master Taíno and slave Paul at MsC 2023
Photo Courtesy of Efraín González

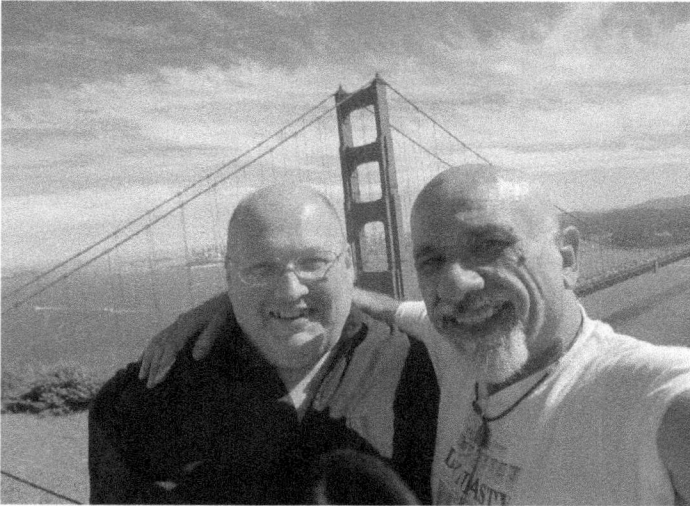

Master Taíno and slave Paul at San Francisco Bay by the Golden Gate Bridge (2015)

Flogging Mother and Son

During the Masters' Weekend offered by the MTTA Academy, I presented the Cathartic Flogging class. During the first decade of the Academy, a slave would receive a flogging during the class; but since 2011, I have begun to ask one of the attending dominants to experience receiving a flogging.

Prior to offering this publicly during MTTA, I was often asked by other Masters and dominants to flog them so that they could personally participate in the experience of being flogged. Oftentimes we would do this right after the Academy ended on Sunday or a few days after.

A female dominant asked sometime later to be flogged to undergo the experience. We planned for her to come to my house on a Friday evening. According to her, she had a very satisfying flogging experience in my dungeon that evening.

Coincidentally, she had a son in his early twenties who was just beginning to explore his interest in BDSM. Several shared friends and acquaintances in the community recommended to him that he should reach out to me.

He contacted me the same week his mother was scheduled to visit, and I agreed to host him, also in my home on Saturday morning, the day after his mother was going to come over. To this day I don't know if he knew his mother was flogged during her visit, nor if she knew her son had come as well.

The son and I spent a full day talking about BDSM and M/s. He was extremely happy with the generous amount of information he had received in just a few hours. Before he left, he requested to experience a cathartic flogging. I agreed; we went down to the dungeon, and I fulfilled his wishes.

In less than twenty-four hours I had flogged a mother and her son, both heterosexuals, both dominants. That was very cool, and the fact that both trusted me with their experiences speaks volumes and humbles me.

I often discuss my belief that many of our sexual kinks are genetic. I believe they come to us through our DNA. We are born this way. We can accept it and be happy, or repress it and be miserable. This story is just another personal observation, where I have seen relatives that are kinky; whether on the dominant or submissive side.

Flogging a mother and a son in less than twenty-four hours is a story I remember well; it is quite unusual, and I cherish it greatly.

My Boots, My History

Early in my journey, I used to wear black hiking boots whenever I would go to the DC Eagle. It was all I could afford at the time. After I pledged to my Leather club, I discovered a cycle shop in my neighborhood carrying Harley Davidson biker boots at a more reasonable price. I purchased my first pair of Leather boots in that store.

That pair of boots became my constant companion wherever I went related to Leather and BDSM. After that, I bought other boots, but that pair of biker boots were my favorite ones for over two decades.

Eventually, I was able to purchase another pair of similar biker boots that I used only for the most formal events.

Then, in the spring of 2010, something unplanned happened. I made the decision to expand my Leather Family beyond my slaves and household. The previous summer, there was a young man in my class "Transitioning from BDSM to M/s" during an event in New Jersey. After the class he approached me due to the topic of my class. He was only twenty-eight years old and had been tying girls up consensually since high school. He felt that there must be something more and understood that was part of what I was explaining in the class.

We ended up at the hotel restaurant talking for a good chunk of time. I invited him to attend and volunteer at MsC 2009. He did and then attended the Masters' Weekend of the MTTA Academy and became my mentee.

That was the beginning of the story of Sir Ross. I realized that he was very serious about our dynamic and was learning fast and following all my advice. All that lead me to wonder if he was the kind of guy I wanted in my family, even though he was not gay, a slave, or a boy. At the time, I did have a slave girl in service to me. Ross was a straight dominant, and I decided to open my family to others who were not my slaves and formally invited him to join the family. He accepted.

Knowing that he was going to have a leather vest with the Leather Family patch affixed to it, he asked me what kind of boots he needed to purchase. I told him that I would let him know. I found out what his shoe size was and realized that my original biker boots would fit him. I developed the idea of passing my boots on to him, as I did have a new pair. I took the boots to get new soles and heels, and my slave David polished them. The result was that they looked like new, not like a twenty-year old pair of boots. I had taken good care of them.

I set the induction of Sir Ross alongside slave Paul for a Sunday afternoon in May, 2010, at my home. Sir Ross came for the weekend. I had the boots ready in my room.

On Saturday night, before going to bed, I looked at the boots and suddenly I realized what I was doing. Those boots had been with me for twenty years since the very beginning of my Leather journey. Those boots had been in every Eagle and Leather bar I have been to in DC, New York City, San Francisco, Chicago, Atlanta, Toronto, Dallas, Phoenix, Los Angeles, Philadelphia, Baltimore, and so many other cities. Those boots have been in Leather bars in Amsterdam, Madrid and Barcelona, Berlin and Cologne, London, Rome, and Buenos Aires. Those boots have been on me many times at MsC, Folsom Street Fair, Folsom East, IML, MAL, South Plains Leather Fest, Southeast Leatherfest, Southwest Leather Conference, Northwest Leather Celebration, Leather History Conference, and many other events. I have worn those boots through innumerable classes I have attended or given.

Those boots had been kissed and licked many, many times by countless men. Those boots had seen their share of a boy's cum and had been licked thereafter. That pair of boots had been pushed against the faces or genitals of many young men during play. I have had a lot of fun wearing those special boots.

Those boots had a history; those boots are my history. And I was gifting them away!

When Sunday came and I performed the ceremony, I made sure that Sir Ross understood I was gifting him an important part of my history. He got it, appreciated it, and embraced it.

As a final thought, I want to clarify that I was not following a preconceived tradition of gifting leather. I just decided to do so when Sir Ross asked me about purchasing boots. I gift leather whenever I want, and it was the right thing to do. I do not strictly follow some of the past traditions, although many in the Community believe there's only one way to gift or earn Leather.

Leather is not what
you wear...
Leather is a way of
living...
Leather should be
in your heart.

Master Taino

A Three-Decade Secret

This story depicts one of the occurrences in my Leather journey that has had the most powerful impact on me. I attended and presented at CLAW 2012. During that event, someone was stalking me, by his own admission. I never noticed.

He attended my classes and followed me throughout the event. A month later, he applied to the MTTA Masters' Weekend and attended that summer. During my Cathartic Flogging class, he witnessed me flogging another Master in the class, and he reached his own catharsis just by watching and receiving our energy. I noticed him and immediately knew he was going to ask for a flogging. I could never have imagined where that would lead or what the Universe had in store for the future.

That Master did ask for a flogging on Saturday evening, and we agreed to do it on Sunday after the Academy was over. During the closing round table, he presented me with a Leather arm band after he had heard me say that I had gifted mine to a junior Master in my Leather Family. He remarked that he had no idea at the time why he had packed that new armband. It seemed the Universe was definitely working on something.

After the Academy was over, we went to my dungeon, where he told me the secret he had carried for more than three decades. He shared the story of being raped by three older guys when he was ten years old. He had never told anyone. I was the first person he had shared what he believed was his shameful secret. After watching the previous cathartic flogging, he realized a flogging experience could help him to heal, as he believed the secret was affecting his Mastery.

I flogged him that evening and twice more weeks later, until he let go of all the inner pain he had harbored for so long.

I am letting him tell the rest of the story in a letter he sent me after the Academy and another he wrote to me and published on his profile in social media.

This is the story of Sir Greg, who later became a member of my Leather Family. Tragically, he and his slave aaron both died in 2015. Personally, I still have a hard time coming to terms with his passing, as he was a strong candidate to follow in my footsteps one day and fill my boots.

But the Universe does work in mysterious ways. His passing opened the door, allowing me to start spending time in Costa Rica and to establish a second home there. I flew back from his memorial in Indianapolis on an early Tuesday morning after a long flight delay. I was scheduled to travel to teach at an event in Atlanta two days later. At the last minute I cancelled my flight and the event. I was not emotionally or physically ready to travel and teach after his death and the following memorial. The funds from that trip would be used months later, allowing me to travel to Costa Rica for the first time in 35 years. That trip saw me open my relationship with EscenaCR and led six years later to my establishing a second home in that Central American country.

Sir Greg tells his side of the story as follows. First with a letter after his initial flogging after the Academy and then in a second journal entry, which he published, detailing how the flogging experience had healed him and had changed his life. I decided to share those writings here to honor him and for this to be part of the legacy of a great man and Master.

At the hands of Master Taíno
by Sir Greg

A cathartic flogging at the hands of a True Leather Master of Masters.

During the Master's Training Academy, I was fortunate to watch a cathartic flogging so close that sometimes I could feel the wind off the leather flogger.

I was seated within seven feet of the Saint Andrew's cross and just to the right of Master Taíno as he started his spiritual and sacred dance or movements, with him and the flogger becoming one. I watched Master Taíno's movements and strikes as if watching a church service, as everyone in the room was sitting in silence with no movement during the scene.

During the course of the scene, I started to become aware that the energy in the room was changing. I slowly started becoming self-aware that I was somehow involved in the scene; as to the feeling — what I later found out to have been the energy being shared and the feeling of the strikes coming off the flogger.

I watched as the intensity continued to build, feeling something inside of me moving in a way that I had never felt before.

During my time in the Leather Community, I have closely watched or casually observed between thirty to fifty floggings at events, parties, or bars, and I had never felt any remorse or feelings from watching these... or any scenes before this one.

During the aftercare, I watched and was still feeling a very strong tie to what I had just witnessed, to the point of trying to hold back, as this of all things had built up and become an emotional incident to me.

I stood back and was waiting for everyone to leave, as I was having a strong feeling that I had never felt before in my lifetime. I had felt the strikes from the flogger, I felt the sadness, and I felt the bonding.

Master Taíno saw that I had or was involved in the scene and that I had a small cathartic event of my own. He stepped to me and with just an opening of Master Taíno's arms and a simple hug, gave me a feeling that I had never felt before . . . a feeling that I belonged.

During this time, he explained that I had had a catharsis from my closeness and the exchange of everyone's energy that had flooded the room.

As the day went on, I kept thinking about the cathartic flogging from our workshop earlier in the day, and it kept coming back to me several times during the rest of the night.

I had never been flogged, had never once even been thinking about allowing someone to control me in such a way, but I kept going back into my own forehead to the strong force that I was feeling within my mind.

I approached Master Taíno, and he already knew what I had to ask . . . and after a couple of words from my mouth, he said tomorrow after the academy is over.

Later that evening, everyone returned to the hotel, and I could not sleep very well . . . I just kept thinking to myself . . . What have I done, and why did I need to experience this spiritual event.

The morning came and went . . . it was a good day . . . but I was wishing that it would last, as at the end of the academy . . . I was unsure what I had asked.

The spirits of the universe and the planets seemed to have lined up on my journey . . . and everything has put me at the place I needed to be at this time in my life.

I had so many things during the course of these days pointing to me and telling me that this is my path and that it was meant to be.

After the end of the day, everyone was being taken to their drop-off points, and we were all saying goodbye. I was starting to feel a strong relief that it was now time.

Master Taíno came over and sat down on the sofa with me, and we talked for a couple of minutes.

He stood up and advised me that we would go downstairs in ten minutes, and he walked away. My mind went wild, my chest started to explode, and I felt like I had just been placed on death row waiting to be killed. Master Taíno came back in ten minutes, and we walked downstairs to his cross.

I stepped into Master Taíno's room, his church, his temple, and my heart was pounding out of my chest, my body shaking, my breathing erratic . . . and I felt like a small child standing before a god.

I felt safe with no fear, but my body was acting up in ways that I had never expected. I was afraid of the unknown, afraid of what was to come.

I was just about to receive my very first flogging, a cathartic flogging at the hands of Master Taíno.

He spoke to me for a couple of minutes and felt my chest as my heavy heart was pounding out of my skin.

The music started, and I followed his instructions to prepare myself as I started to undress. He pointed to a small pad on the floor before him and ordered me to kneel.

I knelt before Master Taíno and looked up into his eyes, I could feel my breath being erratic, and my body was still unsettling up till this time.

After a few moments, Master Taíno was holding or hugging me, and it felt like a very strong and great energy between us, I felt safe and was ready to start my journey.

We both stood up and he led me over to the Saint Andrew's cross with its leather hanging on chains from the restraining points for the wrists.

He was telling me to use my mind, process the pain; it is up to you what you feel and how your experience will take away from this event.

I was standing naked in front of the Saint Andrew's cross as Master Taíno slowly raised my right hand, placing it into the first leather wrist restraint.

He then slowly moved across my body and took hold of my left wrist, as Master Taíno slowly raised my left hand and attached me to the cross with the second leather wrist restraint.

I started saying to myself that this is now up to me, as I was with all my heart a gay Leatherman and kept thinking to myself that I cannot appear weak.

I felt a strong hand touch my left side with the flogger touching and slowly being moved across my back, now softly striking the upper section of my back, warming up the skin, and starting to get the blood flowing inside my body.

I felt a calming sensation coming over my body as Master Taíno slowly but methodically moved across my back with the light strikes as I was ready to start my first experience at the hands of a Master.

The music continued and the strikes started getting more and more intense, but I was never worried about the outcome, as I was feeling more alive than I had ever felt in my life.

I could picture Master Taíno starting his spiritual and sacred dance as the sound of the flogger was in the air.

I looked past the cross and was seeing only the blackness of the walls, hearing the music in the background between the strikes on my exposed back.

I felt a lifting of my body or maybe my soul; my body was ready for flight as I felt my strength increase within my body starting to fly. I was ready to take on the world, and I was still tied.

The strikes from the floggers continued and were changed from one to the next as I felt a rush of energy come across my body, but I did not feel any pain.

I continued to hear the music and feel a slight sting from the presence of the floggers that were growing in the weight of the strikes, causing my body to sometimes drop or lower toward the ground.

I could feel a lifting that felt like my body or even my soul was being pulled away from my body.

I recall raising my head and looking up toward the heavens . . . toward the ceiling of this tiny black room.

I felt the energy or the existence of more than just myself, some kind of power that was growing inside of me.

I felt that I was speaking, but I was unsure of the words or what I was trying, needing, or wanting to say.

But I felt that I was at peace with myself and with the universe, and the energy between us was good.

I recall the music and the striking of another flogger . . . a very strong, powerful flogger as I continued to show the power that I had within myself, standing back up and not being beaten down. I felt my inner strength, and I was strong.

I felt as if a wild beast was coming to the surface, showing itself to me for the first time, and this animal was taking over as I found that my speaking was more of a growl.

I was feeling as if my inner strength or part of my soul was a gray wolf running wild in the woods as part of the hunt.

Now I feel myself being held; Master Taíno was standing between me and the cross, holding me up.

I could feel him removing the leather restraints that had bound my wrists above my body.

As the restraints were removed, I could still feel my hands holding the bars and not wanting to let go for a few seconds as I felt great sadness for a second or two . . . not because of any pain, as I was not feeling pain, but because it was over.

Master Taíno started the aftercare and was still holding me. I could feel his energy filling my body after each breath we exhaled, as we were building a stronger bond that no one could take away from us.

The time passed slowly as I felt weak and found myself kneeling on the ground with Master Taíno still with me, freely sharing this spiritual and emotional journey.

A few minutes had passed, and we stood up. My body was soaked with sweat, and he had me kneel.

He was seated and had again pointed to a small pad on the floor before him and ordered me to kneel.

I knelt before Master Taíno and looked up into his eyes; as he looked into my eyes, I could feel his thumbs running under my eyes on my cheeks . . . starting in the center and slowly moving outwards.

During this time, Master Taíno was telling me that he was pleased, that he had not expected my inner strength as we had used more, much more, than he was expecting that I would have been able to withstand.

He continued with the aftercare and told me that I had been growling during the cathartic flogging and how I would raise back up with my body, signaling that I was ready for more and more.

Our energy continued to pass freely between us as my face was pressed into his chest and near his heart, and I was feeling a bond that I had never experienced with anyone else in my forty-three years on this earth.

I am still processing everything that happened and searching for the reasons . . . but I felt like I belonged and that I had a feeling that I was safe, and again that very strong feeling that I belonged.

As this journey today, I had started on my knees, kneeling before Master Taíno and feeling as a small child standing before god . . . I have now returned full circle and been reborn as a Leatherman kneeling before a Leatherman.

After a few moments, Master Taíno told me to get dressed, and my inner feelings are that I am now ready to further my journey.

I never looked at my back while at the house, as we were running a little late to get me to the airport.

Master Taíno had his slave david take me into town and drop me off at National Airport.

On the way there, I kept thinking that I wanted to see my back, to feel the torn and abused skin, to see the marks left by Master Taíno.

We arrive at the airport and after quickly making it past security, I find myself searching for a restroom . . . a bathroom stall . . . somewhere that I could remove my shirt and use my cell phone to take a couple of pictures and to reach around and touch the welts.

Over the past couple of days, I have had time to process more and more from this, and I am still searching for the reasons that we were brought together.

I have something telling me that there is more of a reason — that something is still missing, but in my mind I already know that Master Taíno will be the only person that I will allow to flog my back.

A cathartic flogging, Sunday, July 24, 2011, at the hands of a True Master of Masters . . . Master Taíno.

Sir Greg – Indianapolis, Indiana
Master's Academy class XVII

My Dominant Side To Control Was Born
(Journal Entry published in social media)

I wish to start off by saying that this experience did not make Me gay . . . I have been gay for as long as I can remember . . . knowing that I was slightly different from all the other boys in My class. This experience has made Me stronger, and My Dominant side to Control was born.

I had been searching and My realization that something is there, and it is a strong yearning for knowledge and finding the mindset needed to fulfill and realize My true abilities and to become a stronger leader for the community.

I am a strong Dominant ... I do find that a caring and loving dominant does run very deep within My soul with My own beliefs of how a caring, loving, and nurturing leadership encourages the sense of family and of belonging to something larger than oneself.

I am seeking to find my true path on my journey.

I have felt that this is somehow the correct path for my journey, as I have been thinking that something has been missing in my life, but still searching to find my true purpose.

I am now in the process of presenting classes and workshops / round tables on domestic violence and abuse, that is so hidden and not spoken of in Our community.

I remember an incident from My childhood, as I was playing about a mile and a half away from My parent's home out in the country, near the railroads at the age of twelve or thirteen.

On this day, I found out that some people are not kind. I was grabbed up by three males between the ages of what I would have guessed to be eighteen to twenty-five years of age, and at that point in time ... they took away My childhood within those three long hours at their hands.

I was taken into the woods near the railroad track, where I was beaten and struck so many times that I could not count, but at that age I could have never imagined anything could get worse ... but it did.

I was picked up off the ground and held down between the "Y" branch of a small tree, where I was then stripped of all my dignity as they took off all of my clothes, and as I was being bent over between the branches of the tree, each of them started having their way with My mouth and ass.

After about three hours, the deviant conduct, sexual battery, and beatings stopped; one of the males then went into the cornfield and returned with an ear of corn that they shoved into my ass, causing Me to bleed for almost a week.

I was too ashamed that I felt that I had let this happen and never told My parents, or anyone else for that matter ... even though they had been out looking for Me, trying to find Me, during the time this was taking place near the tracks.

I have never told anyone close to me what had happened on that day . . . over thirty years ago, but that has a strong background as to who I am and how I feel about not being in control or even thinking of giving up some or any control to anyone over me.

That is the reason that I felt scared to death as I was willing / trying to submit to Master Taíno and his flogger.

I did feel a very strong bond and energy between us ... as I have stated before, "a feeling that somehow I belonged." That is why I could barely breathe, and my body was shaking prior to my cathartic flogging.

That was the first time on Sunday, July 24, 2011, that I can remember after this incident that I had willingly given up control over My body.

I have been seeking somewhere to belong, as I have been finding my place, but always before having a fear or a feeling of anxiety that I needed to remove from my past.

I have been hiding for so long in this life, that this one horrific event has controlled and made me part of what and who I am at this point in My journey.

I am sorry that I was not all forthcoming with everything from the start. But as I write this I am still opening up and feeling more at ease, but still with a strong feeling of being damaged goods.

During the MTTA Academy, as Master Taíno pointed out several times, emotions are part of who We are and how You freely showed that even You have sadness in your life, but giving each a chance to build up Our own confidence. I hope You will continue to guide me along My path and the respect before I revived this history and past.

I wish to Thank You, Master Taíno for becoming My Mentor and My Master of Masters.

Thank You - Master Taíno

Respectfully Yours in Leather Brotherhood,

Sir Greg - Indianapolis, Indiana

Straight Firefighter

An interesting thing that has happened during this journey I am on is that I have had multiple encounters with submissive, heterosexual men. Of great interest to me is that each one has a different story, interests, limits, desires, and fears. Usually, they are comfortable enough to surrender to a gay dominant for their needs. Unfortunately, many gay individuals do not like to play with straight folks.

This story is about one straight submissive male, who happened to be a firefighter in the area. Contrary to the firefighter stereotype, this boy was not tall or big. He was a young, smooth, medium-sized guy, with a strong and beautiful body. He was an adorable young man with an awesome smile.

When he reached out to me, he told me his hard limit was anal sex. I discovered that he was a great kisser. Very often, straight dudes are the opposite — interested in anal sex and no kissing. He reached out to me because of my experience and knowledge in BDSM, and not for physical attention or attraction.

The firefighter was very open to BDSM scenes and wanted to try everything. Through several encounters he became a regular. He experienced spanking, flogging, nipple play, CBT, bondage, and more. One time, I told him I wanted to introduce him to electro-stimulation. He greatly enjoyed the Violet Wand. Then, I told him he should try my ErosTek TENS unit, which included a butt plug and cock ring as attachments. He agreed, and he had a blast. It was the first time he had ever experienced something inside his ass.

I knew that he was interested in exploring with younger dudes. When a younger bisexual Master friend of mine visited for a weekend, I called my firefighter and asked him if he wanted to play with both of us. He came in a hurry. Upon arrival, he got naked and was tied up on my bondage table. I connected the electric butt plug and cock ring and began to do some electricity on him, while my buddy began to do work on some of the boy's pressure points at the same time. I liked to play with this boy because of his great reactions. While he was experiencing our play, I asked him if he was reacting to what I was doing with the electro or to what my friend was doing with the pressure points.

His replies were one or the other.

As our ministrations grew more intense, I asked him again what he was feeling, my buddy or me, and he screamed,

"Both!!!" We all had a good laugh.

Months later, Sir Greg, a young member of my Leather Family, was visiting. I thought it would be a great opportunity to give my firefighter an invitation to come over. He had been working overnight and was at my home by 9 a.m., right from work. This time, among other play, we put him on the sling and connected him again to electro, both the butt plug and the cock ring. He really liked electro. Then came the big surprise when the boy told me that he thought he was ready.

"Ready for what?" I asked.

"Anal sex," he replied.

I told him that there were two of us, and he would have to take us both. He agreed. Of course, I went first. I wanted to be the one to pop his cherry. It is very special for me when I penetrate straight subs who are still anal virgins. I took his virginity, something I hoped he would never forget, either the experience or me. Sir Greg followed, being the second to penetrate the young man. His experience was intense, especially for a virgin. I will never forget his face after everything was over. He wore so many mixed emotions on his face after his experience, as though he were riding an out-of-control merry-go-round.

Straight men feel safe with me. I am adamant about letting them know that I acknowledge and respect the fact that they are straight, that they are attracted to chicks, and that I have no intention to try to "convert" them into turning gay. Many gay people do not understand this and think that if they are sexually involved with men and do not accept that they are gay or bisexual, then they must be in denial.

I have learned from straight men that mostly the younger guys who are into alternative sexuality are secure in their heterosexuality and want to explore their sexuality in other ways. That is why I make a distinction between sexual orientation (who you are) and sexual activity (whatever you want to do).

There is nothing
more rewarding
than making a
difference in
someone's life.

Master Taino

The Girls Brought The Boy

As a gay man, I sometimes like to be a bit of a smart ass to have some extra fun. During Folsom Street Fair 2011, I had been flogging all day. I have been doing this at the Panther Prowls booth during the full 2010s decade.

A beautiful young woman from Los Angeles asked to be flogged, and I complied with gusto. She had previous experience, and I was able to give her a pretty good flogging.

Afterwards, she asked if I would flog her female friend, but warned me that she did not have any prior experience at all. I assured her that it was not a problem and flogged the friend as well.

Both girls hung around the booth, seemingly happy to be watching me work. Sometime later, I noticed a very handsome, tall, young man talking with them in a very friendly manner. It was obvious they were friends.

Keeping an eye on the young man, I asked the girls how they were doing after their experience. They responded that they felt great.

"Is he next??" I asked them, as I really wanted to flog his back.

The girls convinced him that I was a good experience and he should try it. They literally brought the young man over to me.

I chatted briefly with the young man, who was heterosexual. My intuition told me he would do very well, even though he had never been flogged before.

I took a few minutes to explain a few things to him about what I would be doing. I then proceeded to give him an amazing flogging all over his wide, beautiful back.

The flogging was quite intense for someone with no experience. His catharsis was priceless, and he left a very happy camper.

As a gay Leatherman, I have no problem doing BDSM with straight folks, female or male, particularly with flogging. Sometimes, like that time, girls can bring you the boy you really want to flog. It's a memory I cherish. I still remember fondly that afternoon at the Fair.

On a Castro Sidewalk

As I have done for a quarter of a century, I attended Leather Week and Folsom Street Fair 2011 in San Francisco. I never imagined that I was going to have a memorable end to that week.

On Saturday afternoon, I was talking with some friends in front of the Starbucks in the Castro gayborhood. I noticed a young man sitting inside, staring at me. After noticing him several times after that, I decided to go in and figure out who the young man was and why he was staring at me like that. We ended up having a nice chat. He was from Los Angeles and had just graduated from college in San Francisco. He was a straight man with some conflicts concerning his female relationships. He talked about his admiration for the gay community. I shared with him who I was and the fact that the next day I would be flogging all day at Folsom. He was intrigued by my flogging and agreed to stop by the booth where I was going to be the next day.

On Sunday, while I was flogging, I noticed him among the onlookers, but when I finished that session, he was gone. After the Fair was over, I drove back to the Castro to have dinner, and afterward I stopped by the Starbucks for coffee. While I was enjoying my latte, the boy showed up. He said he was still interested in receiving a flogging. I told him that I had been flogging all day, and he left. When I asked what he was doing the next day, he said that he was taking an early bus back to Los Angeles. I was about to tell him that he had lost his chance but then I realized where I was — in the Castro. Anything can happen in the Castro. Anything does happen in the Castro. So I told him that my car was parked in front of the Edge Bar, my floggers were in the trunk, and there was a wide sidewalk on Collingwood Street next to the bar. I told him I could flog him there.

He enthusiastically agreed, and we walked there and picked up the floggers. The space was perfect, and the brick wall of the Edge helped the setting. It was dark at 9 p.m. I spent some minutes explaining to him my philosophy concerning flogging and what I would expect from him. I proceeded to remove his shirt and put him against the huge brick wall. I placed my hands over his back, sharing my energy, and then started flogging him slowly to see how he would react. After a good warm-up, I realized he was processing well, so I began to increase the intensity until I took him to a good catharsis.

After we were done, I turned him around with his back to the wall. The boy was flying, and he was looking at me intensely with the same big eyes that had called my attention to him the day before at the coffee house. Without consciously thinking about it, I stared back into his eyes and slapped his chest with both hands. He reacted with a big groan, which I loved. I kept slapping his chest hard, and he groaned louder and louder. His reaction to the impact on his skin was amazing and beautiful, and our eyes kept connecting with intensity. I was pouring tons of energy into his chest with my hands, just as I had done on his back with my floggers. He was loving it.

More than a decade later, I still have great and vivid memories of this experience, because of the huge connection I was able to make with a young straight boy, and the fact that all this happened at 9 p.m. on a sidewalk of the iconic Castro gayborhood.

I am still in contact with the young man, who later spent some time in the Navy and is now back in Los Angeles. I could never forget him! That evening was memorable — flogging at night on a sidewalk in the Castro. Priceless!

We create our path and develop ourselves as leaders by joining, being proactive, and being doers... with hard work, ethics, commitment, dedication, and love for our community.

Master Taíno

A Powerful Day

The weekend was supposed to be just another academy for slave girls. I never imagined how that Saturday would enhance my life. Yes, that particular Saturday ended up being a very powerful day like no other.

This academy for slave girls had a common denominator: most of the participants had experienced abuse at some time in their relationships. There was one girl who was suffering in an abusive relationship at the time she was in attendance.

After the Cathartic Flogging class, all of them wanted to experience a flogging. I knew it was going to be powerful and emotionally draining for all of them.

Because I literally do a flogging marathon during the MTTA Academy weekends, we developed a protocol at that time where I would provide the first couple of minutes of aftercare to the participants and then pass the participant to Lady Lynette. She would finish the aftercare while I took a rest, preparing for the next flogging.

I remember that morning, while resting between floggings, I took *The Washington Post* to relax my mind. I noticed an op-ed from a male intern in DC, who wrote about having been sexually abused as a child. He was begging society to take care of children and not protect abusive and negligent institutions. That was during the time the Penn State sexual abuse scandal was unfolding.

So here I am, dealing with the abuse suffered by the girls, and at the same time being affected by the abuse at Penn State and the clamor of that young intern. I have always been outspoken against any type of abuse, but I really get upset when the abuse comes from adults that are entrusted with children. I have been entrusted with children many times in my life and have never crossed that line and hate when others do so.

It came time for slave Celia's flogging. She was the female in an abusive relationship at the time. Her flogging was intense; I could hear her talking to her abuser and saying she was not going to allow it anymore. What surprised me was the effect the experience was having on me. Every time I do a flogging, the energy involved in the scene always affects and sometimes drains me emotionally. But this time it was different. My whole body and mind became a mess, and I felt emotionally overwhelmed. My body was shaken and my mind confused. It is very difficult to try to describe what I was feeling.

I let Lady Lynette continue the aftercare of Celia. Lady Lynette noticed my demeanor and asked if I was okay. I could not respond and left for my room immediately. However, I passed Master David in the hall, and he, a psychologist himself, also noticed something wrong and asked me what it was. I lay down on my bed, resting and trying to figure out what was happening. Half an hour later, I did not even want to get out of bed; but I had to do so, as there were two more girls waiting for their flogging experience, and I needed to do my job.

After I was finished, it was lunch time. I sat at the table, and Master David again asked me what was going on. I could not speak and retreated again to my room, where I spent the afternoon resting and trying to figure out what was happening to me.

Finally, I figured it out that afternoon. I have spent many years helping people, assisting them through catharsis to work past experiences that were still hurting them, their unresolved issues damaging their bodies and hearts. And who was absorbing all that crap? The Master holding the floggers. It had finally caught up with me. My strong feelings against abuse, so exposed that day, may have contributed as well.

At the same time, I was helping Celia turn her life around. She returned home after the academy and ended her abusive relationship. Months later, she met a young Dominant, with whom she started a M/s relationship, eventually got married, and had a baby girl. Later, they both asked to be accepted into my Leather Family, and they were welcomed.

Months later and after another flogging experience, we had at an event in Atlanta. Celia sent me a letter with her thoughts and feelings about her experiences during my floggings, and I share it here with her consent:

> Master Taíno,
>
> I have sat down to write you several times. My letter has had the middle and the end completed and stared at. I have felt sheepish and shy at my own words, but they come from the heart. As I write this, I realize that the hardest part is often the beginning. You have become such an integral part of my life. You have given me so much that I sometimes feel as though anything I could give you would be paltry in comparison; but I know you. The connection I have with you is beyond what I had ever thought would have been possible of a teacher and student.
>
> You are more than a teacher or friend to me. What I feel for you is, even for me, hard to put into words. You have a permanent place within my heart, and I do genuinely love you.
>
> I was a broken woman when I came to you and the Slave Academy. I was emotionally cracked and physically beaten by people in my life that should

have just loved me. They should have protected me. They should have cared for me. Not even knowing me, you gave of yourself to me.

You gave me a cathartic flogging. It was painful. I had to face the misery and the suffering that my own partner was putting me through. I sobbed and I screamed. I fought and beat myself against my bonds as you flogged me, urging me to let go. Why? Why have so many hurt me? I give so much of myself and so many have given me back nothing but grief in return. I deserve more. I deserve better. I deserve love and kindness. I deserve a life of nurture and warmth. You struck me again and again on the cross, coaxing, begging me to let go, until I screamed out my own redemption. I would never allow this hurt to poison my life again. We collapsed together. Shaking and sobbing, you held me, and I knew I was not alone.

I never expected to do this again. Seeing you at SELF I was excited, but I had no idea you would ask me to scene with you. It was hard to restrain my excitement. I felt honored! I was unsure of what to expect when you restrained me, but as soon as you touched your hand to the small of my back, I knew whatever you had in store for me would be powerful. I smiled as I felt the flogger fall against my back and shoulders. I was right.

It was electric. The flogger was not a tool of pain or misery, but an extension of your arm and your energy. You wielded it with a controlled intent on pulling something to the surface that needed to be released, and with each strike I felt your energy flow into me, and mine pour out to you.

This time was different. I was not in mourning or in anguish. Flashes of my past catharsis with you spilled across my mind like shattered bits of glass. Instead of lamenting over what was broken, I rejoiced. In tears I could not help but erupt in laughter. Here I was bound in the center of a noisy dungeon, the air thick with bad music and the heat of too many bodies packed into a room, and with tears spilling out of my eyes I was laughing. I have overcome what I had once thought to be impossible.

Your floggers struck my back, and the sordid embers of my fire were stroked and urged back to flame. I could feel my heart lift, and my soul overflowed in mirth. I have been reborn. I am brighter than I have ever been, and nothing in this world can stifle me. I am a phoenix. Though I blaze blue and ferocious, I choose not to burn. There is so much in this world that I want to touch, that I want to be a part of. And now I can.

Without the first catharsis I would have never thought it possible to overcome what I have and to be able to laugh as you renewed my spirit a second time.

I love you Master Taíno. I am a strong, powerful, and an overwhelmingly happy slave. I am surrounded by the love I have been waiting for, and you helped me to realize just how much I deserved it.

Thank you so much for sharing your gift with me.

With Love,
Slave Celia

The walls of shame
and embarrassment
are coming down, and
people are free to
explore their
sexuality.

Master Taino

"I Can Cry"

A young, heterosexual dominant man asked me to give him a mentoring session. As this is something I have done many times previously, I agreed. On a Saturday morning he came to my home, and we discussed BDSM, M/s, kinks, cathartic flogging, and a myriad of related topics for the entire day.

He was very intrigued by the cathartic flogging that I teach and that I have such a great passion for. I was not surprised at all when by late afternoon, he asked if he could experience cathartic flogging by my hand.

We descended to the dungeon in my basement, where we talked a bit more about it. When he was comfortable and ready, he took off his shirt in preparation to begin.

Benedictine monks' Gregorian chanting filled the space over strategically-placed speakers, bringing an aura of tranquility, calmness, and spirituality to the cathartic flogging ritual.

The flogging started slowly, warming up his back, which had never felt that type of impact. After a time of measured and slowly intensifying flogging, he did reach his catharsis and began sobbing out of control. Then I heard him saying over and over, "I can cry, I can cry."

When he came back from where his catharsis had taken him, I asked him what he meant. He then told me his story. He had not cried since he was a young child. He believed that he had lost his capacity and his ability to cry and express his emotions. The cathartic flogging experience had allowed him to cry and to express his feelings by sobbing for the first time in years.

Why do I cherish this story? Through cathartic flogging I can guide a person through the use of impact to let go of life-altering issues they may hold inside by releasing those negative emotions through crying and sobbing.

With this young man, his issue was his inability to cry. I was able to help him accept that he can cry and that it is okay to have a good cry once in a while. Those floggers always do a good job.

Straight Dom

One summer I received an e-mail from a young man in his early thirties requesting some BDSM training. The individual said that he was a straight dominant who wanted to serve me for a weekend as a way to learn more about himself and his dominance. That is an approach that I like and respect, as I too submitted to another dominant early in my journey to learn the basics of BDSM.

We were unable to put together a full weekend, but we met twice on Wednesdays. The first time he visited I was alone in my home. I decided to give him specific instructions that would make the start of the encounter more fun as well as add some protocol; it was also a way to determine how serious he was.

I instructed him to let me know when he had parked his car on my street, which he did. I told him the front door was unlocked and he should enter the house, lock the door, strip his clothes off, and kneel, facing the door with his head bowed and hands behind his back. This is something I have done countless times with other trainees.

While he did that, I was in the kitchen, where he could not see me. When he let me know that he was ready, I came into the foyer, and I was in absolute awe of what I was looking at. He had the most perfect body a person can only dream about. He was tall and built, with a wide smooth back and beautiful round buttocks. His haircut let me know that he was a military guy, something he later confirmed. When I stood in front of him and raised his head, I realized that he was a very handsome man.

We then started talking, so he could share his interests with me, and I could tell him what I could do for him.

Eventually, I took him to the dungeon, where we started playing. He could not do spanking or flogging, as he had a physical scheduled for the next day at his base. We got into the hot tub for more talking, and eventually we went out for dinner.

He expressed his interest in experiencing anal sex for the first time, and I was more than ready to honor his request. Unfortunately, his hole was very tight and there was no way to get inside.

When he returned for the second time, we did the spanking and flogging. During the flogging session, I very quickly realized something was wrong, so I stopped and asked him. He stated he was having a hard time with the flogging, because, as an officer, he teaches young military guys how to repel torture. It made it difficult for him to get into the right headspace needed to receive a flogging. I understood, so we moved on to something else.

I recommend that he try electro-stimulation, but I warned him that one of my electric toys required a butt plug. After using a violet wand on him, I proceeded to prepare him for my ErosTek unit. I placed the electric cock-ring on him and was able to shove the butt plug up his ass. Even though he remained tight, it was easier after lubing him well to push it inside. That was fun.

By the time we were done, and I was removing the butt plug, I knew how much I wanted to penetrate him myself. I thought that after the electro experience, two things could happen. Either he would be sore because it was the first time he had gotten something up his ass, or the electro-stimulation would loosen him up and he would be able to take my cock. The latter worked, and I was able to take his virginity with enormous pleasure.

I think he learned how his girl feels when he takes her from behind. Contrary to most straight subs that enjoy being fucked, he did share that all he felt was the desire to poop. I was extremely happy and fulfilled to be able to take him and give him that probably once-in-a-lifetime sexual experience.

It was a great and fun experience, as it was different from the usual. I gained much respect for him, as he was able to do what he did in order to learn and become better at his craft. Besides the BDSM and sex, we spent a good amount of time talking about BDSM and M/s dynamics. He was a good listener.

That was an encounter that I will cherish in my memories, as he is probably one of the hottest men I have ever played with. A specimen of a man, handsome and built on the outside, and a kind, genuine man on the inside.

I believe we have the responsibility to study and know the history lived by many others before us.

Master Taino

Short Flogging Stories

During my kinky journey, I have flogged countless numbers of individuals, many for the first time in their lives. The following are a handful of some special sessions that made for very good memories.

Tiger Tattoo

I visited New Orleans in February of 1997 for a Pantheon of Leather event. At the Phoenix Bar I ran into a Master I had met the previous month at Mid- Atlantic Leather (MAL) Weekend in DC.

Our conversation ended up being about flogging, as he had seen me flogging at the MAL host hotel. During the chat, he mentioned how he had witnessed an intense flogging scene at a public play space in San Francisco the year before. What really impressed him was that the recipient was not bound to a cross but standing firmly with his hands in front of him. I asked him if the guy receiving the flogging had a huge tiger tattoo on his back. He was surprised by my question and responded in the affirmative. Then I told him that I knew about the tattoo because I was the one doing the flogging. Needless to say that he was very surprised by this coincidence.

St. Michael

Way back in the year 2000, I met a young man from Baltimore who was interested in our unique dynamics. Of course, I introduced him to flogging. I was surprised when he took off his shirt the first time. His back was decorated with a huge tattoo of St. Michael, the patron saint of my hometown. Here I was ready to flog over a St. Michael. I had never imagined doing something like that. Yes, the tattoo got some extra color. I remember as well that I had removed a small necklace from his neck to put a chain collar on him. At the time I hung that small necklace on the Leather banner where I keep all my event pins. Almost a quarter of a century later, the necklace is still there, always as a memory of the boy with the St. Michael tattoo.

Screaming too much?

During the event in Washington, DC, called BR (Black Rose), I met a straight young man; we subsequently ended up engaging in an intense flogging scene. The boy was screaming his lungs out during his powerful catharsis. A dungeon monitor reached out to me asking if I could make the boy be quiet. BDSM is about expressing and letting go of your emotions, and the boy was doing just that.

I was really surprised by the request of this monitor. He may have been clueless about what BDSM is all about. The boy's intense catharsis was a way for him to grieve the recent ending of his first kinky relationship.

Zen Meditation

At Folsom Street Fair 2011 in San Francisco, I flogged a local young man who practiced Buddhism. He reached a good catharsis and left after the session. Later that afternoon, he returned to let me know that I had taken him to a peaceful place that he could only compare to the Zen meditation he often practiced. Yet more evidence of the spiritual aspect obtained during a cathartic flogging experience.

Not A Show

During Folsom Street Fair in 2015, a handsome Filipino-Italian young man, attending his first Folsom, showed up early on my flogging booth. That lovely young man named Paul (like my current slave) became the first boy I flogged that day. There was a very special connection and energy between us. I remember telling my slave Paul that if the first boy was that good, it was going to be an awesome day.

Later that afternoon, the new Paul returned and told me that he cherished his experience with me. He wanted to ask why other flogging scenes he saw during the Fair looked like more of a show. I was glad that he noticed the difference, and I gave him my card. Paul e-mailed me the next day and visited us in Virginia two months later. Since then, we have become very good friends. I have been to his place in Dallas, and he even visited me in Costa Rica as well.

Club de Osos

When I visited Buenos Aires, Argentina, in November, 2019, I held a class at the Club de Osos (Bear Club). I also attended several social events there, including a class on tango dancing. With my best friend in the country (I had met him back on a previous visit in 2005), I spent a Sunday afternoon at an outdoor pool dwarfed by two high terraces and surrounded by ivy-covered walls. Within that unusual scenario, I flogged my buddy on one of the terraces for the first time since 2005, with the mostly vanilla crowd as witnesses. That was very cool, as the vanilla folks were intrigued and respectful of what they had witnessed. After that we returned to the pool, followed by a good *mate* (a typical Argentinian tea-like drink).

Jumping to the Opportunity

At the TESFest event in 2022, I offered my class on Cathartic Flogging. The young guy monitoring my class was extremely efficient, and I always appreciate good service. During dinner that evening, I mentioned to Sir Edgar how impressed I was with the efficiency of the monitor and the fact that I would like to reward him with a flogging. Sir Edgar made a call to someone who knew the young man. I learned that when he was approached about my interest, he was told that if Master Taíno wanted to flog him, he should jump at the opportunity. He sent me a text, and we agreed to meet at the outdoor hotel courtyard dungeon at nine o'clock p.m., after his volunteer shift for the event ended. We had a very good initial talk and then an intense flogging experience together. When his aftercare was completed, we kept talking about BDSM and M/s until midnight.

My Floggers

I knew I had an interest in flogging early into my journey. That interest developed into a passion. During the early 90s I started my journey in the Leather Community. I was still raising my adopted kids, and money for BDSM toys was scarce. I managed to purchase my first flogger during an auction at Leather Pride in New York City in 1994, the same weekend the Gay Community celebrated the 25th anniversary of the Stonewall Riots. I waited until the end of the auction to bid on a flogger, after most people were gone or had already spent their money, so I was able to get it at an affordable price. Unfortunately, I lost it during one of the famous Dungeon Dances in D.C. It just fell from a Velcro holder I had it on. That lead me to purchase a cheap one.

One Saturday night, after a long night at the DC Eagle, I found a flier from the Leather Rack, the leather shop in Washington, DC, on the windshield of my car. They were offering any item purchased the next day at half price. I wanted to take advantage of that opportunity, and on Sunday evening I went to the Rack and purchased a beautiful deerskin flogger for half price. I loved that one since the very first moment I had it in my hands!

Months later, while I was in San Francisco for Folsom Street Fair, another leather store, A Taste of Leather, was having its twenty-fifth anniversary sale and had many items discounted. I jumped at the opportunity and purchased my second flogger at half price —a shorter bullhide with an identical handle to match the deerskin flogger.

During Folsom a year later, I ran into a flogger shop owned by a lady named Sarah. I had heard about her business called Sarah Lashes. She saw both floggers hanging from my belt and asked how I liked them. I told her that I loved them. She then told me that she had made them. At the time I did not know that I owned two floggers from Sarah!

While attending IML 2000 I wanted to purchase a third flogger from Sarah. I remember I was thinking that I wanted a flat braided one. I got to her booth and told her what I wanted. She told me that IML was her last show, as she was retiring due to having developed carpel tunnel syndrome. Sarah went over to her display and picked up a heavy bison flogger and told me, "Master Taíno, this is what you want."

With a "Yes Ma'am," I got my third flogger, an extremely heavy and beautiful bison flogger.

That same year I returned to San Francisco for Folsom. I wanted to find Sarah, so I could purchase at least one more flogger from her. However, her website, phone, and email were all down. During a visit to Mr. S, I asked the owner if he knew about Sarah. He told me that she had given them all her remaining inventory. Oh my — "there were Sarah floggers right here," I thought. I went directly to the flogger rack and in a few minutes I found myself with three floggers in my hands — a soft deerskin, a cow, and a third, which was the most unique flogger I had ever seen: a heavy cowhide with one-inch wide laces. "Nasty shit!," I told myself and that became its nickname: Nasty Shit.

Three floggers were a lot of money, but I realized that it was now or never, and so it had to be now. I went to the owner, whom I knew, and asked him to convince me to take all three. He gave me a good price and it was a done deal. Later, I returned for another one that resembled a leather razor strap, with the unique Sarah handle. Now I had seven floggers from Sarah in my collection.

Years later I was presenting my Cathartic Flogging class at an event in New Jersey and mentioned my story about

Sarah at IML. That evening during a reception, an elderly lady attending the class showed me a small, flat-braided flogger, which I identified by the handle as being made by Sarah. When I tried to return the flogger to the lady, she told me it was a gift, because nobody would appreciate it more. Now my Sarah collection was up to eight.

Finally, a good friend from NYC, Master Tip, passed away in 2018. I asked his partner if I could purchase any floggers Master Tip had that were made by Sarah. His partner ended up donating everything in Master Tip's dungeon to MTTA and told me that if among the floggers I could find what I was looking for, they were mine. And that I did. I found two. Now my collection includes ten Sarah floggers.

Most of them have seen more than two decades in my hands, and I love each one of them. My Sarah floggers have become acquainted with many, many backs over more than three decades.

In addition to the ten floggers from Sarah Lashes, I purchased a beautiful cat-o-nine tails flogger at an auction during IML in the early 2000s. However, a friend was also bidding on it and was aggravated that I got it. He claims to this day that I stole his flogger. I keep telling him that all I did was outbid him.

There are special floggers that I appreciate very much which have been added to the collection.

When my mentor Master Steve retired, a lot of his stuff was auctioned off at Southwest Leather Conference, the event he founded. There I found a tomcat which was originally owned by Guy Baldwin and then gifted to Master Steve. That tomcat was owned by the two most influential people who had showed me the way into my journey as a Master. I wanted it very badly. Someone else also wanted it badly, and we engaged in a bidding war. I finally got it for close to $500. After the auction, the other bidder asked me out of curiosity how far I was willing to go, and I told him that I did not know, as some things in life are priceless and that tomcat was one of them. When I leave this world, I want that tomcat to go to the Leather Archives with the names of the three people who had owned it previously.

I have a flogger with rubber barbed wire tails which slave llamb made for his owner, Lady Lynette, my Leather sister. After her passing in 2015, slave llamb gifted that flogger to me. Then, after Master David, my Leather big brother passed in 2017, his Leather Family presented me with one of his floggers during MsC.

I am proud of my prized collection of floggers, my babies, which have given me so much pleasure and which have touched so many lives in a very positive way.

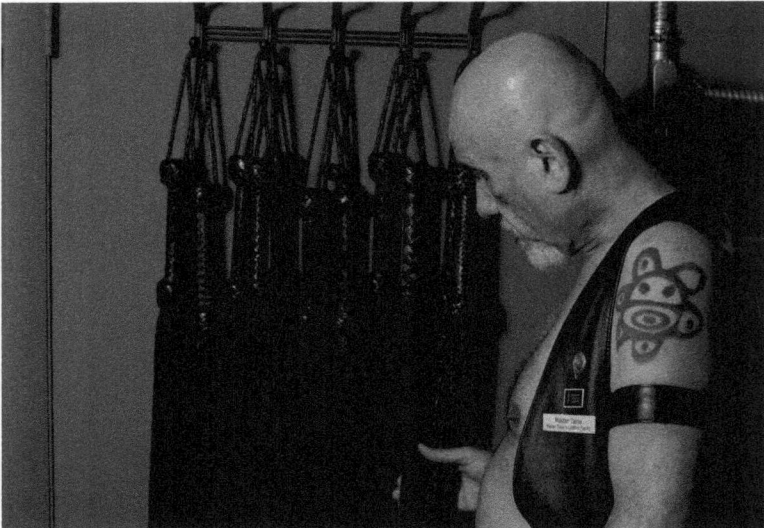

Photo Courtesy of Yali Molina

The Cross

Back in early 2002, I was invited by my mentor, Master Steve, to be a guest instructor for Butchmanns Academy in Tucson, Arizona. A Saint Andrew's Cross dominated Butchmanns' huge dungeon. This cross captured my attention, and I took pictures to have a similar one created at home.

A friend from Frederick, Maryland, who made beautiful paddles, was commissioned to build my cross. That very cross was in my home dungeon for over two decades.

I am spending most of my time in Costa Rica now, so I sold both steel cages, a sling, and the cross. I kept a folding cross that slave Paul gifted to me several years ago to be our "traveling cross."

Letting my old cross go brought up a lot of mixed emotions. As I strolled down memory lane, I started remembering many individuals that I have flogged on that cross. Mostly young men, but many women, too. Mostly gay, but some straight, some bi, and trans as well; mostly submissives, but also many dominants. Hundreds is more likely, possibly even a thousand. I am not sure, but there have been many. Behind each flogging there is a story, and behind each story, a treasured experience.

For nineteen years I flogged most of the students at the MTTA Academy who asked for it, especially after attending my Cathartic Flogging class. Most remarkable is the immense majority of those who were tied up to my cross that *did* reach catharsis during their flogging experience. So many tears nourished that cross. Not all cathartic reactions end up in tears; many also reach catharsis by laughing out of control. According to many who have experienced catharsis on the cross, the experience somehow made an impact on them and changed their lives. That is the rewarding part of what I do: the Universe has taught me that there is no better reward for a human being than making a difference in another human being's life.

That cross has seen it all. From participants coming to terms with their authentic selves or succumbing to their surrender, to letting go of deep-seated issues like abuse, abandonment, toxic families, and toxic relationships, the end of relationships; from grieving the loss of a loved one to liberating themselves from the inner pain these situations created within them.

I am glad that the cross was bought by someone who understands its history and its ownership and who will care for it accordingly. The cross is still nearby, as the new owner is a friend and neighbor.

That cross will always be part of my Leather journey and history.

Costa Rica

During my lifelong journey upon this Earth I have learned to let the Universe take me where I should be. This is how I found myself in Costa Rica.

I first visited back in the late seventies when I was in my late twenties. I fell in love with the beautiful Central American country and returned two more times. I took my parents with me on my second trip. In late 1983 I relocated from my native Puerto Rico to the U. S. mainland and did not return to Costa Rica for more than three decades.

In 2013 I received an email from Master Jota, who was forming a BDSM group in San José called EscenaCR. He asked me to write a message in Spanish for the group's initial publication, which I did. It was not the first time I have been honored by Latin American kinky leaders reaching out to me through the internet.

In summer 2015 I needed to use up some funds from Southwest Airlines before they expired. I decided to plan a week-long visit to Costa Rica directly following MsC. I let Master Jota know about my trip, and he immediately invited me to do a presentation for the group. During MsC, Master Francis, a member of my Leather Family, decided to join me for the trip.

Master Jota and the Costa Rican folks, known as *Ticos*, were very happy to have us. Master Jota even provided a young slave boy (young man of consenting age) to serve me during my stay. Master Francis and I offered a general class that included a flogging to the boy who was in service to me.

During that trip I fell in love with the country all over again. I already had a task to write a book in Spanish. The grievous string of deaths within my Leather Family that I had suffered during the previous months (slave david, Lady Lynette, slave aaron and Sir Greg) created a sense of urgency within me to begin the book project. I knew I had too many distractions at home to interrupt my concentration, so I decided to rent an apartment for a month in San José and dedicate myself to writing the book.

Master Jota helped me find an apartment, and four months later, in January, 2016, I was back in the country to start writing the book. While doing that, I also had the opportunity to offer another class to the EscenaCR group. I realized that there was an immense interest in BDSM among young gay men, who reached out to me through social media apps. When my stay ended I had not finished the book, and so I returned for another month in the winter of 2017.

At the same time, my relationship with Master Jota and the incipient kink community was growing. During this visit Master Jota took me to be interviewed for a radio program. Master Jota was a young man in his early 40s, extremely well-educated and intelligent, with great plans to develop the community there. Unfortunately, he passed away during a surgery later that year. When Master Kai, the other leader of the group, called me to give me the sad news, I told him that the best way to honor Master Jota's memory was to work hard to achieve Master Jota's dreams. I challenged him to do just that but had never imagined that I was going to be part of that process.

I returned to Costa Rica in the winter of 2018. Master Kai had put together a full day teaching event for me. I ended up doing four or five classes that day. This is when I met another Jota, a young law student in attendance. We connected immediately, and I became his mentor. Later that year he attended MsC and stayed a couple of weeks at my home. He was eventually invited and welcomed to become the first Costa Rican member of my Leather Family.

Meeting Jota became a huge turning point in my life, as he was an activist and began to arrange for me to present classes to different groups, including psychology students at the University of Costa Rica. Due to this, I continued traveling to San José every winter.

Back in early 2019 Master Kai told me about his desire to have a MAsT Chapter in San José, but he thought they would not have enough people to do so. I assured him he would have enough and assisted him in the process. By May, 2019, MAsT San José was holding its first meeting, and I was happy to be in attendance.

In the winter of 2021, while I was in Costa Rica, I agreed with the new MsC hotel back in the U.S. to cancel the event again because of the pandemic. I did not want to go back home, where I had spent nine months in 2020 in isolation, never leaving the house. It was then that I decided it was the right time to get my own apartment in San José and spend more time in the country.

By May, 2021, I had my own place and had increased my participation with classes on BDSM and M/s. I travel three times a year back and forth, but I have been spending more time in Costa Rica than in the U.S. My flogging reputation has grown fast, and I have become the flogging teacher there. I am happy to flog whoever asks me to flog them, whether male, female, gay, straight, bi, gender fluid, dom, or sub.

The following year I was able to arrange American and Canadian M/s educators to present at the MAsT San José Chapter while visiting the country. Those presentations were in English, as most of our community speaks that language. I was so happy to have them, not only so the local folks could experience different points of view, but also so my guest presenter friends would have the opportunity to get to know my people and understand why I am so happy living in this beautiful country.

Some of the Costa Rican Community leaders have been able to attend MsC during the last few years. Not only have they have attended, but they have volunteered, becoming staff, and have even given presentations. MsC is part of their lives now. Many others are looking forward to being able to attend as well.

On his first trip to Costa Rica, Master Taíno with the late Master Jota, the founder of EscenaCR, Fabián, and Master Francis.

In 2023 I was able to take a suitcase containing some heavy toys, including a body bag, a strait jacket, and four sets of iron shackles, to Costa Rica. With those toys, I was able to put together a class on bondage without using ropes. It was awesome to see a crowded room of young men and women trying out all the toys I had brought — toys that were just gathering dust in my home in Virginia. It was very rewarding.

The Community in San José has grown incredibly. They are constantly offering classes on Shibari, flogging, spanking, electro, fire play, and many other forms of play. I am very happy to be able to help them and to be there. Besides being a teacher I have become a mentor to many young men and women. That is even more satisfying for me as a teacher.

The Universe guided me to this beautiful country, where I have found happiness in the last stages of my life. I am living a quiet, tranquil life. I am enjoying spring weather all year long, meeting cute boys and at the same time continuing my journey as I teach others about BDSM and M/s. This time I am teaching to *mi gente*, in my native language. This has been the best "retirement" I could dream of. *Pura Vida!*

History isn't just the past. History is the past, the present and the future. We have to remember and honor the past, build the present and prepare the path for the future.

Master Taino

On the Fast Track

During my time in Costa Rica in my later years, I love to offer basic BDSM and M/s classes to the "*Ticos.*" In late November of 2022 I was giving a basic class to a group of about twenty-five predominantly young people. Among the attendees were a couple of students from the University of Costa Rica. He was twenty-two and she was twenty. He jumped into volunteering for everything, from nipple clamps to electro. When time for flogging arrived towards the end of the class, we were short on time, so I invited him to receive the flogging, as he seemed to be well into it. He did so well that I was surprised, and by the end he was flying.

While I was packing my toys at the end of the class, he came to me and left his number. I never imagined that little paper with his name and phone number on it would be the start of a kinky relationship. I called him the next day to see how he was doing, and by the end of that call he agreed to visit in a few days to explore more.

A few days later Luis and his girlfriend showed up at my door. After more talk about BDSM he was ready for a session. Something I teach newbies is that BDSM is a mental activity, not only a physical one. The brain controls the body, and if you set your brain correctly on your goals when surrendering to a BDSM experience instead on the so-called pain, your body will respond accordingly. And this boy did that, as I have seen not too often.

On that first private experience, Luis took a level of intensity usually seen in people with years of experience. He was having so much fun exploring flogging, spanking, paddling, caning, electro, CBT, TT, and so on. Nobody could believe he was a total novice. And that started a kinky relationship that led to many play dates.

A couple of months later, I invited Luis to be part of a new class where I emphasize that if we put the sex aside, BDSM allows us to play, connect, exchange energy, and reach a level of intimacy with people whom we are not necessarily compatible with sexually by gender or sexual orientation. At the end of that class I performed what was his third cathartic flogging and took him to a level of intensity which projected him into a deep trance. Attendees could see the deep connection that a gay Master and a heterosexual sub can achieve through BDSM.

Luis has become one of my mentees, not only for kinky instruction, but for life issues. I gifted him his first paddle. I admire and respect him for feeling so comfortable exploring BDSM with a gay dominant a half century his senior. He has become one of my many kinky grandchildren in Costa Rica. Luis is one of a kind — a very special young man who keeps exploring and learning more and more in this amazing kinky world.

Here is his side of the story:

My introduction to BDSM
by Luis

I was invited by my then-girlfriend to participate in a class about BDSM. We had talked earlier that it was something she had explored, and I wanted to explore it, too. So, there was a mutual interest in the class with Master Taíno. For me everything was very interesting: all the floggers caught my attention as well as the electric toys.

I was extremely excited, so when Master Taíno asked for a volunteer for flogging, I immediately welcomed the challenge. I wanted to clearly prove that I wouldn't miss the opportunity. Since I don't have any problem with public nudity, it seemed like the perfect opportunity.

I followed Master's instructions, and without any problem, I stood in my boxers against the wall. Master gave me instructions to breathe well and have good posture, and upon feeling the first blow the word I can describe for the moment would be pure excitement. I immediately felt very excited by what I was feeling, and it was definitely something I expressed with my breathing and behavior. He increased the intensity using stronger floggers, and I couldn't stop enjoying it more and more.

I must say that it was an incredible experience for me. My girlfriend was a little worried about me. I even realized that she was also breathing hard when I received the impacts. We had a connection there, and the looks from the spectators only filled me with joy. Everyone enjoyed it. They were also very excited, but no one was as excited as I was myself.

Of course, I wanted a full session, so when the class ended, which wasn't long after that, we approached Master Taíno to ask for more information, and we shared contacts. It wasn't long before I had my first full session with Master Taíno, and the experience was magnificent. The intensity was much greater, and I enjoyed it a lot. For the second session, even my girlfriend joined in, and she also enjoyed it a lot. It became a therapy for both of us; we were learning together, and that united us more as a couple and brought us closer to knowing what we both liked.

When my relationship ended, I was a little absent. I didn't know how to play with Master without having her as support, as since she had become my unconditional company. I felt strange not having her, but after a while I decided that coming back would be good, and that's how it was. I have had several sessions with Master, and I even feel that after each one I can feel better about the loss of my incredible relationship.

Age Gap

Being attracted to young adult men means the older I get the wider the age gap becomes. I have been lucky to run into young subs eager to learn, who are at the same time very attracted to older men — the Daddy type, or, as I have been called in Costa Rica, the Leather Grandpa type. In Costa Rica I have found a good share of boys interested in BDSM and submission.

In late 2022 I met this boy who was just eighteen and the age-gap was fifty-four years. This was the widest age gap I had ever had with a young man. He lived with his mother and grandmother without a father. Consequently, I believe I filled his own natural need for a father figure. Also, being that young, he was a virgin.

When I meet newbies, I immediately teach them my philosophy: dominant and caring. This is my own personal mantra in terms of my BDSM practice as well as in my Master/slave relationships. I like to dominate, but I do care for those I dominate. This boy got it right away.

Inherently, he did so many things right. After we had a long conversation in which I explained what BDSM and submission are and how I practice them, I earned his trust, which is essential for good play and a good relationship to take place.

He enjoyed every bit of it. He had discovered a new world. He had discovered a lot about who he was and has returned repeatedly for more. It remains interesting and unusual that such a young boy loses his virginity both in sex and BDSM at the same time.

I am going to complete this story by sharing what this boy wrote to me after our first encounter:

Good evening, Master Taíno,

I hope this email finds you well. I write tonight to elaborate on my first experience entering the BDSM and submission scene with you as ordered.

Overall, I quite enjoyed the experience from start to finish. The warm welcome was greatly appreciated in helping to calm my nerves around the whole situation, and the familiarity with which you explained the terms and told me stories gave me confidence and even more interest in the experience.

I really liked the combination of dominant and affectionate energies that you exhibited during the process: the hair pulling, spitting in his mouth, grabbing my balls, and telling me to kiss your body in particular made it much easier for me to enter a submissive space, while the words of affirmation, kisses, and hugs helped me feel safe in this situation.

On the BDSM side itself, I really enjoyed the different types of play. I felt from the beginning that the exchange of energy gave us both a good idea of the level of roughness with which the play was going to be carried out. At no point did I feel scared for my safety even when restrained or asking for the intensity to be reduced, when I felt overwhelmed.

I enjoyed all the types of play we tried: the spanking with the hands and with different paddles was a very pleasant start (I should add that that area is still marked at the time of writing this message, which makes me very happy). Regarding flogging, I also enjoyed it a lot, knowing that it was your favorite; I entered that scene with a lot of excitement, and even though I had to ask you to stop at a certain point, it is an activity that I want to experience again. I also found the play with sharp objects very exciting, since I never felt in danger, but I did feel out of control, which again helped me test my trust in you.

The strongest pain I felt in the entire session was the one that originated from the nipple clamps. Frankly, at certain points it became overwhelming, but the rest of the things I was doing to the rest of my body helped me cope. (At the time of writing this email they still hurt a little. It's exciting to feel the pain when touching them and remember the session).

In conclusion, I very much appreciate all the knowledge and details you showed when preparing me, asking for my consent, during play, sex, and aftercare, and I look forward to continuing this process.

Yours in submission,
(Name withheld)

NEXT GENERATION

They will build their own history and walk their own path. They will continue enriching our Leather History.

Master Taíno

Leather Grandpa

"I have learned so much from you. In my heart you will forever be my Leather Grandpa. I hope to keep learning from you. Thanks to you I am in love with flogging, teaching, and so much more. Thank you for being here."

Orc Alpha
San José, Costa Rica
Oct. 10, 2022

That was written by one of my Costa Rican mentees (and now the newest member of my Leather Family) in a social media posting after attending her first Master/slave Conference in Washington, DC. When I read that and saw her calling me her "Leather Grandpa," I realized that was where I was at this point of my life, living into my seventies. I love it, and I ran with the title.

Yes, I love being a Leather Grandpa.

Yes, I want to keep caring for my kinky boys and girls.

Yes, I want to keep teaching them.

Yes, I want to continue helping them discover their kinks, BDSM, and their M/s D/s relationships.

Yes, I want to guide them in their journey.

Yes, I want to make a difference in their lives.

Because the community in Costa Rica is mostly integrated by younger folks in their 20s and 30s, I have begun to refer them as my "Leather Grandchildren" (*Mis nietos y nietas*).

Back in the 80s, a counselor advised me to fulfill my mission. That advice has guided my life since. Now, taking care of my Leather grandchildren may be the last of my missions in this long life I have been blessed to live.

There are several personal reasons and stories why being called a Leather Grandpa touches my heart in very special ways. Both my grandfathers passed before I was born. When I was a child, I would get upset because most of my friends had grandpas and I did not. So I "adopted" as my grandpa a retired teacher who lived next door, and he embraced me as his grandson.

Later, in my 40s, I was able to visit the village of my Spaniard paternal grandfather in Northern Spain. I even slept one night in the house where he was born and lived until he turned sixteen, before he emigrated to Puerto Rico. He never returned to Spain. I "got to know" him by visiting his village in search of my roots and ancestry, even though he had died a half century earlier.

Wondrously, three of my adopted sons gifted me with four beautiful granddaughters who made me their grandpa.

I am a firm believer in the mantra, "Love makes a Family," framed and embroidered by a former slave and found at the entrance of my home. The people whom we learn to love and who love us throughout our lives become family. This is what I have experienced in my retirement years in Costa Rica. I do love and care for those in our local kink community, and they have also given me so much love and care in return.

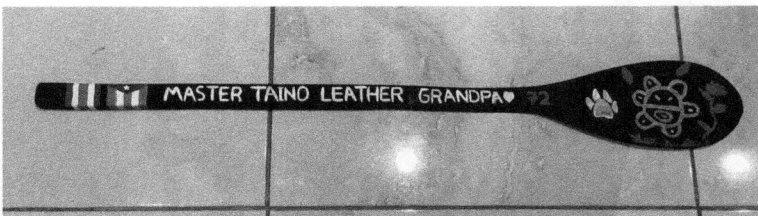

This is what I call family. The Universe has allowed me to be a Leather Grandpa for my chosen family. I am humbly honored and proud to be a Leather Grandpa.

www.ingramcontent.com/pod-product-compliance
Lightning Source LLC
Chambersburg PA
CBHW031125020426
42333CB00012B/235